Trains

CUTAWAYS

SERIES EDITORS:
Erika Balsom (King's College London)
and **Genevieve Yue** (The New School)

"This new series of small-format books focused on cinematic motifs, themes, and devices represents something new and exciting in English-language writing on film." —**Dennis Lim, Artistic Director, New York Film Festival**

"Featuring some of the field's most exciting scholars and critics, Cutaways is a welcome addition to film writing. The series promises to expand the ways cinema is conceived, consumed, and received, in ways that parallel the contemporary situation of cinema." —**Sarah Keller, author of *Anxious Cinephilia: Pleasure and Peril at the Movies***

Cutaways is a series of pocket-sized books by and for movie lovers. Each volume offers a journey through the history of cinema guided by a single motif or formal device. Featuring original writing by film scholars and critics, the books create a space for intellectually engaged and broadly accessible cinephilia.

Trains

Genevieve Yue

FORDHAM UNIVERSITY PRESS NEW YORK 2027

Visit us online at www.fordhampress.com.

For EU safety / GPSR concerns: Mare Nostrum Group B.V., Doelen 72, 4831 GR Breda, The Netherlands, gpsr@mare-nostrum.co.uk

Library of Congress Cataloging-in-Publication Data available online at https://catalog.loc.gov.

Printed in the United States of America

29 28 27 5 4 3 2 1

First edition

For S, who wanted to sit next to me on a train

Contents

Introduction: Departures 1

1. How It Feels to Be a Woman on a Train 17

Itinerary: London to Venice 34

2. Ends of the Line 40

Itinerary: Los Angeles to Rhinecliff 62

3. Phantom Rides 71

Itinerary: Shanghai to Hong Kong 91

4. Strangers on Trains 97

Acknowledgments 111

Notes 113

List of Figures 119

Index 121

Trains

Introduction
Departures

The history of film is intimately tied to that of the train. They sometimes loop around each other, and other times run parallel or overlapped tracks. Arguably the two most important inventions of the nineteenth century, the cinema and the train also resemble each other in their mechanical organization, with both filmstrip and railroad track held in place by standardized widths. Lynne Kirby has suggested that the train, "as a machine of vision and an instrument for conquering space and time," is film's "mechanical double."[1]

These are machines that make people and images move. They frame, disorient, and enchant. In the nineteenth century, they were vehicles for a modern mode of encounter. Suddenly a landscape appeared blurred from the window of a train, or through the aperture of a camera lens. There is regularity to both—they operate according to published timetables, in predictable increments—until they give way to the unpredictable: slow-downs, interruptions, derailments, and occasional combustions.

For Marian Martin (Joan Crawford) of Clarence Brown's *Possessed* (1931), the train that rolls through Erie, Pennsylvania changes everything. For one, it draws a line between the world she lives in, and the one she longs for. She likes fellow factory worker Al Manning well enough, but marrying him would spell only more of the same, dreary life. At twilight she wanders along the tracks. A train comes in, and she steps to a platform to meet it. Each passing car presents a sight more enticing than the last: porters laying out silver on white tablecloths, a maid ironing lacy undergarments, an elegant couple dancing, then dipping for a kiss. It's like an unfurling diorama, or a movie. When the caboose arrives, a man in a tuxedo stands at the railing, holding out a martini glass. "Have a drink?" he asks, and the train miraculously stops, as if its entire purpose has been to offer Marian this invitation. The man continues. "Looking in? Wrong way. Get in! Look out . . ." The order of the scene is now split not only according to a class division, but the perspective from which one looks. Having more means seeing more, and more fully. The man is headed to New York City, and he beckons Marian to ride with him. For now she accedes only to a pour of champagne. Until the moment she touches the glass, everything is like a dream. All her desires have been paraded before her, just for her. But in this moment of contact, just when it seems the spell will be broken, it's confirmed to be real. Slavoj Žižek has called this scene "cinematic art at its purist."[2] Like many Depression-era films, *Possessed* offers the fantasy of a better life. In this moment, it all but guarantees its concrete realization, delivered by a train.

The train is a pervasive model, analogy, and subject of film. The motif is so common that it begins to appear overdetermined. Silent cinema is unthinkable without the image of a train, from Auguste and Louis Lumière's *Arrival of a Train at the Station* (*L'Arrivée d'un train en gare de La Ciotat*) (1896) to the nascent expression of continuity editing in Edwin S. Porter's *The Great Train Robbery* (1903). Early tracking shots came by way of the phantom rides popularized in turn-of-the-century Britain, short films recorded from the front (the "cowcatcher") of a locomotive rolling through a familiar or foreign landscape, and which gave viewers the sensation of travel without ever leaving their seats. Later, the train became a staple of genres like the western and the works of directors like Alfred Hitchcock, Wes Anderson, Satyajit Ray, and Chantal Akerman. Dating back to 1912, the "coming attraction" trailer, so named because it was hitched to the ends of feature films like a caboose, became commonplace by 1919.[3] Cinema even invented its own small train, the camera dolly (likely a derivation of the word and shape of a trolley), which was used for the weightless glides of Kenji Mizoguchi's camera, or revealed by Jean-Luc Godard in the opening sequence of *Contempt* (*Le Mépris*) (1963). The prehistory of film is also marked by the train: In 1873, Eadweard Muybridge devised a system to document a horse's gallop through a series of rapidly exposed photographs, answering the question of whether its running feet ever fully leave the ground. His motion studies, along with those of Étienne-Jules Marey, who admired Muybridge's work, would become foundational to the mechanics of the motion picture camera. Muybridge's employer Leland Stanford was a racing enthusiast and owner of the Central Pacific Railroad, and in another bit of historical continuity, Stanford was the one to hammer the golden stake that joined the western and eastern portions of the United States' first transcontinental railroad. In the Soviet Union, meanwhile, the train was seen as a potent political tool that could aid cinema in reaching and radicalizing the outer, often illiterate reaches of the revolution.

There is no such genre as a "train film." Taïna Tukunen calls it a "moveable category" that may in fact be uniquely adept at traversing genres.[4] Using the metaphor of the train car itself, she observes that the energies bound up within the space and time of the railway voyage have a tendency to exceed them. "Despite attempts by railway and film production companies alike to classify and compartmentalize," she writes, "train interiors provide suitable sites for shocks, startling encounters and plots."[5] The train is a catalyst for action, drama, and romance. It summons the unexpected and the contingent—the new. In other words, the train generates cinema.

This book was written in the imaginative dust blooms of a racehorse's gallop. It does not take the convergences of film and train history as a foregone conclusion, but looks to spaces where things might have turned out otherwise: unintended stops, intervals between film frames, momentary reflections caught in the glass of a window. Against the exploits of heroes who battle their foes on the roofs of speeding locomotives, or race to rescue maidens tied to the tracks, this book sits with passengers who are absorbed in thought, who sometimes doze, or whose movements have no easy rationale. It lingers with the children of *Killer of Sheep* (Charles Burnett, 1978) who play in a barren yard, clouded by the dust of a passing train that will travel farther and faster than any of them. It listens to the symphony of wheels and screeches above the muffled voices of passengers, some of whom sleep in the train bathroom or on cardboard laid out on the floor, in J. P. Sniadecki's *The Iron Ministry* (2014). It dwells, not with the robbers who break into a moving express car, but the view of the passing forest offered by its open door, in *The Great Train Robbery*. It travels with cars and engines built for nineteenth- and twentieth-century transport, and that still rattle well into the twenty-first. It tracks abandon and abandonment.

I offer this book as a feminist study. In using this term, I do not primarily mean films that feature women, or that were made by women, though those certainly appear in this book, in abundance. Nor do I go out of my way to avoid the great train directors—people like John Ford, David Lean, Alfred Hitchcock, and Yasujirō Ozu—though when I revisit their films it is from a sidelong way. Feminism, here, is about method. It affords a certain way of looking at film history that is otherwise unmarked or unavailable. This position looks back to the foundational moment of the 1970s, when the introduction of feminist analysis allowed for a critique not just of patriarchy, but all forms of oppression and inequality. Over time, something of a generational rift emerged. In 1976, four editors left *Women and Film*, which they saw as too narrowly focused on "the question of sexual difference as originally formulated," to found *Camera Obscura* in order to examine "questions of difference more broadly defined, equally invested in analyses of race, ethnicity, nationality, sexuality, gender expression, and generation as it is in analyses of gender."[6] Feminist method, as I take it, flourishes in precisely these kinds of departures. It does not abandon its original concerns, but uses them as occasions to step into new spaces and sensations. It makes visible the moments after or astride a crisis. It prioritizes looking, reaction, and thought. It retrieves, from within the history of film, moments of quiet surprise and reflection. It patiently waits for what may appear after the dust settles.

I write in the wake of feminist rupture, because, for me, there is no other way to write. None of this book's questions could have been arrived at without feminism, and none of its imagination would have opportunity to exist. I describe the scenes that have stayed with me; they are like views from a train window. Some of them seem to incline with a mood or feeling, as when a character in Ermanno Olmi's segment of the omnibus *Tickets* (2004) admits, "It's almost as if the train feels a bit like me and is hesitating." More than a few of them involve Barbara Stanwyck. Many of them, in ways that I will not elaborate on further, extend my own memories of drifting and desiring on the train.

Of the earliest films ever shown to an audience, only one comes with a legend. First exhibited in 1896, among Louis and Auguste Lumière's catalogue of "views," a term borrowed from still photography, *Arrival of a Train at the Station* appeared in programs that included a crowd of people leaving the Lumière photographic plant in Lyon, members of the family dining al fresco, a prank involving a garden hose, and a boat bobbing out to sea. The film with the train was the only one that had the power to shock. Allegedly, the sight of a steam locomotive's propulsive, z-axis thrust caused viewers to duck, panic, swoon, and even stampede.

Though scholars, most notably Tom Gunning, have worked to debunk the more sensationalist claims, it is clear that the Lumière train was more than a mere view.[7] Instead it enacted, through film, what Wolfgang Schivelbusch described as the "machine character of the railroad," where "motion was transformed into movement through space by the combined machinery of wheel and rail."[8] Film delivered the train, and it did so perilously close to the viewer's body. Audiences saw—felt—movement: an immense, unstoppable force.

Or so it seems in Maxim Gorky's account. In his review of an 1896 Lumière program in Nizhny Novgorod, Gorky disparages the medium's quality of verisimilitude, which was "not life but its shadow." He writes as though he were recounting a nightmare, replaying each film, each jarring transition (all of which occurred between films, as these were single-shot films) with a sense of dread. The details suggest a level of violent fantasy consistent with later action and horror films, and far less with the genteel bourgeois subjects in the Lumière catalogue. When he gets to the train at La Ciotat, he imagines it crashing into him:

> Suddenly there is a click, everything vanishes, and a railway train appears on the screen. It darts like an arrow straight toward you—watch out! It seems as though it is about to rush into the darkness where you are sitting and reduce you to a mangled sack of skin, full of crumpled flesh and splintered bones, and destroy this hall and this building, so full of wine, women, music, and vice, and transform it into fragments and into dust.
>
> But this, too, is merely a train of shadows.[9]

This last line can be read in two ways: On one hand, the train is the paradigm of cinema's spectral nature, the privileged metaphor for its uncanny vitality. On the other hand, the addition of "too" and "merely" indicates a kind of monotony, as though this spectacle, a synecdoche for cinema itself, is just another disappointment in a life already full of them.

(This coming from a person who chose for himself the name "Gorky," meaning "bitter.") There is a fatalistic undercurrent in both interpretations. Sometime after viewing the Lumière program, Gorky confirmed his dismal attitude about the new medium by writing a short story in which a woman commits suicide after watching little Andée Lumière gobble a biscuit in *Repas de bébé* (*Baby's Breakfast*) (1895).[10]

There is a scolding quality to Gorky's words, which are too knowing to fully surrender to the terror he evokes, and to which the mythical spectator capitulates. He reserves the target of his disdain for the end of the essay, when he invokes the Russian marketgoers and pleasure-seekers who "thirst . . . for the piquant and the extravagant." For him, it is no accident that the new medium was first exhibited in Nizhny Novgorod at Charles Aumont's, a well-known brothel. To satisfy the whims of "loafers," he wryly surmises, films will soon develop more sophisticated methods of delivering pornography and depravity. Crank though he was, Gorky wasn't so far off the mark.

The same Lumière film appears in Martin Scorsese's *Hugo* (2011). During a flashback sequence, Georges Méliès (Ben Kingsley) recounts how he happened on the screening at a British fairground. When the fateful train arrives, the tentful of ladies, gentlemen, and children draw a sharp, titillated gasp, followed by nervous laughter. Méliès, the magician and inventor, is not looking at the screen, but the device. As he explains, he built his own machine after the Lumières refused to sell him one of their own. So begins another track on which film history was set in motion.

Hugo was a box-office flop, in large part because of its marketing as a children's film. Though Brian Selznick's novel

The Invention of Hugo Cabret had been a bestseller, its film adaptation was more invested in the story of Méliès, one of the earliest and most imaginative filmmakers. Audiences who came out for a family-friendly 3D spectacle were rightly confused when it turned out to be about movie history. But the film is inextricably both of those things.

Hugo knits together the story of an orphan who, by some mysterious gears of fate, comes into the family of an aged Méliès, now a cantankerous toymaker. Through several intricate machinations, the arrival of Hugo (Asa Butterfield) restores to Méliès memories of the life he once had. After a chance encounter with a film historian, Méliès is eventually recognized as a pioneer of the medium, and his works are retrieved and restored by the French Film Academy. The latter is perhaps the film's most fantastical creation: In 1931, the year in which *Hugo* is set, cinema had hardly any regard to its own history, much less a film library, film professors, or silent film festivals of the sort that Hugo and his friend Isabel attend. The first film library was not established until 1935, at the Museum of Modern Art, in New York. Meanwhile, preservation efforts of the era were haphazard at best. Robert Daudelin describes film archivists of that time as "romantic pirates; working secretly and in isolation."[11]

In the film, it is the train that occasions the initial encounter between Hugo and Méliès, and sets the trajectory of their converged futures. This is announced in the film's opening, when the still-dark screen is punctured with the sound of a train whistle. Then, through clouds and snow, Paris appears from above, its traffic pulsing like gears in a clock or an engine. In a long, unbroken shot—an especially audacious example of Scorsese's oners—we dip down into a train station, glide along the tracks, then lift up to the central clock face, where, inside the number four, the wide eyes of twelve-year-old Hugo peer out.[12]

Hugo winds the station's clocks, a job he has taken over from his recently deceased uncle. He toils in secret to avoid the station inspector, who would send him to an orphanage if discovered. In his modest apartment deep in the recesses of the station, Hugo works to repair a mechanical man that his father left unfinished after perishing in a terrible accident. Like the croissants he sneaks for his meals, he occasionally palms parts from the toy stall run by Méliès.

Unsurprisingly, Hugo dreams of the train. The film contains a reference to a famous train derailment in the Montparnasse Station. On October 22, 1895, a train's brakes failed and it crashed through the wall of the station, landing on its nose in the Place de Rennes. Hugo encounters this incident as a nightmare. In it, he hops onto the tracks to pick up a small key, realizing too late that a speeding train is headed toward him. He ducks. The train hurtles over him, then flies off its tracks. It swerves wildly through a kiosk and a shoeshiner's bench before bursting through the exterior glass. In a right to left movement that matches the composition of the Studio Lévy photograph of the Montparnasse accident, the engine car crashes into the street below. We know it's a dream because Hugo sits up in bed with a jolt, in the way that only ever happens in movies.

As with many train films, there is a collision—of sorts. In another train-like arrival, Hugo approaches the toy stall from down a long corridor. Méliès is apparently asleep at the counter. Stealthily, Hugo reaches for a mechanical mouse, but Méliès grabs his wrist. Hugo drops the toy, which breaks on the floor.

Méliès pulls Hugo back to him and doesn't let go. The actions of the early scene—two bodies colliding, a broken toy, and the old man holding onto the boy—will repeat in the film's climax, which also recapitulates Hugo's nightmare. Once again, Hugo jumps onto the tracks. This time, the mechanical man has fallen there, and Hugo is attempting to retrieve it before it is crushed by an approaching train. He underestimates its speed, however, and at the last moment, he is lifted up by the station inspector. Before being carted off to the orphanage, Méliès appears, joined by his wife and adopted daughter. He steps forward to embrace the boy. "Monsieur," he says gravely, "this child belongs to me."

The anticipated collision, the one narrowly averted, becomes the occasion for the family to come together. Méliès is restored to his rightful place in film history, and Hugo is no longer an orphan. After the calamity, or because of it, everything is set right. Just as it is in the founding myth of cinema: The terrified spectators of the Lumière train nevertheless remained firmly in their seats for the next 130 years and counting.

The Lumière train also makes an appearance in Ignacio Agüero's 1988 documentary *One Hundred Children Waiting for a Train* (*Cien niños esperando un tren*). Agüero's film follows a group of children enrolled in a film workshop run out of a church in Lo Hermida, an impoverished neighborhood on the outskirts of Santiago. Over the course of several months, the children watch films and learn about the invention of motion pictures, from the illusion of movement produced by the thaumatrope to the projected image of modern-day cinema. Their teacher Alicia Vega announces *Arrival of a Train* as one of the world's first films. She runs it twice. The first time, as the camera cuts away to a view of the neighborhood and the Andes just beyond it, we hear only the clatter of the projector. Then it returns to the children's illuminated faces as they watch, their excited chatter filling the room. (Their reception is much warmer than Gorky's). In the second instance, the image of the train fills the screen. This time, when there is a cut to the children, they are watching in silent awe. Their varied reactions undo the myth of the terrified spectator: There is no one way to view the film, and there can be many situations in which to see it, even within the same room. From within this little chapel, with one excursion outside it, Agüero's movie does no less than rewrite the history of film.

Like *Hugo*, an early moment in *One Hundred Children Waiting for a Train* includes the sound of a train whistle: a call to board. This precedes the first question Vega poses to the children, namely, what films they have seen. They write down their answers, which appear in close-up: never, no, I have never been. Instead, as revealed in interviews, they largely work, helping their parents sell items in the market, or collecting scrap cardboard. Both kids and parents imply that going to the cinema is a luxury they cannot afford. But for Agüero, cinema is a crucial site of social existence from which these children have been excluded. Its apparatus has even been turned into a weapon of the repressive Pinochet regime. When Agüero asks whether they had ever been filmed, a girl recounts an audio recording that was made while her parents were out. Her older sibling adds that the secret police had come to their home, asking questions about their parents' jobs, and whether they had a basement. The youngest confirms that she too had been questioned. She was six at the time.[13]

The children draw scenes from movies they watch in the workshop. When Laurel and Hardy remove their hats, the kids doff their own cardboard bowlers at the screen. They make paper versions of pre- and early cinematic devices like a flipbook and a kinetoscope, and bring them home. Everything

they learn, they take into their hands. Their parents, meanwhile, can't remember the names of the toys. "Something like anthropologist?" guesses a father, perhaps indicating something about the type of filmmaking that usually happens in their neighborhood. "Thaumatrope, zoetrope," says his eight-year-old son, proudly. All of this is play, and it is also deeply serious.

The workshop is in many ways building toward a train, of a sort: The children draw a series of large photograms that they join together under a long red tablecloth, and parade outside the church. Vega dons a whimsical caterpillar head to lead the group. They carry images they have made for a collective film. When, previously, they discussed what topic to select, the children overwhelmingly voted for a street protest Agüero had filmed for *This Is the Way I Like It* (*Como me da la gana*) (1985), and which they watched during the workshop's lesson on documentary. The class sets to work drawing democracy activists throwing stones at police, constructing barricades, and dragging an injured comrade to safety. "This is the protest and this is the woman dead in the street," says a small girl with a giant grin. Undoubtedly the children have already witnessed or sensed this kind of violence around them. Cinema gives their experiences tangible form. In their small hands, it becomes a tool for making sense of their world.

At the conclusion of the workshop, the children are bussed into Santiago to visit a real cinema. Their excitement is infectious—the kids all but tumble over the seats. As the curtains part and the lights go dim, we hear the film's very first sound, the clacking of a hand-cranked camera, a sound not unlike that of a moving train. There is a subtle cut from the theater screen to a close-up, not to a Chaplin film or some other recognizable classic, but a new film made by the children, one of their own arrival at the theater. It is as though they were seeing themselves onscreen, advancing one photogram frame at a time.

The moment recalls a passage from Frantz Fanon's *Black Skin, White Masks*, in which he writes about sitting in a theater waiting for a movie to begin. "I cannot go to a film without seeing myself. I wait for me. In the interval, just before the film starts, I wait for me."[14] Though Fanon is lamenting the stultifying clichés of Blackness onscreen, Kara Keeling reads in his words a moment of potential resistance to cinematic convention, both formally and politically.[15] For the children of Lo Hermida, this potential is realized, if only in cinematic form. In Agüero's telling, the history of film has been leading up to them, to these children whom Vega describes as Chile's most vulnerable people. In the film's final shot, back in their neighborhood, a train whistle can once again be heard.

At the time of its release, *One Hundred Children Waiting for a Train* was restricted to audiences over the age of twenty-one. I can think of various reasons for why this might have been, but I'm most persuaded by this scene in the theater, this depiction of seeing oneself as the central actor of a film. This, to me, is Agüero's most radical gesture—one negatively expressed in the perverse logic of banning school-aged children from seeing themselves onscreen, as if allowing a six-year-old to imagine that kind of power were dangerous. I would like to hope so.

1

How It Feels to Be a Woman on a Train

The first time the woman says her name, a train whistle obscures her voice. Across from her in the dining car, the younger woman (Margaret Lockwood) who has just introduced herself as Iris shakes her head, indicating that she's unable to hear. Her new acquaintance (May Whitty) smiles, and traces a word on the window. "FROY," she says, both reading and repeating. "It rhymes with joy!" As the women speak, the word disappears into the sunlit landscape, then returns when something passes near the glass, too blurry to tell: a row of trees or another train, perhaps.

Alfred Hitchcock's suspense thriller *The Lady Vanishes* (1939) is anchored by this sign of Miss Froy's presence, a discrete mark on a foggy window. Though undeniably tangible, it appears only under certain conditions of light. Because of this, it wavers as much as Iris's certainty about her companion's existence. Her doubt, it turns out, is considerable, given the concussion she's suffered, a prolonged nap, and a train full of people insisting, in the words of a psychiatrist on board, that Miss Froy is nothing but a "vivid subjective image . . . or some past association . . . subconsciously remembered." Later, the chance sight of the word is what convinces Iris that Miss Froy is very real, and in real danger. The camera holds on the window long enough for us to see the name fade from view.

Train glass bears the sign of someone having been there, like the smudge of a previous passenger's face. At the same time, glass is a lens, something to see through. As it sharpens focus on what is farther away, it obscures what is more immediate, including its own surface. Glass, like cinema, can play a game of hide and seek. It offers an image that is often only fleeting, or barely perceived. According to the train's speed, the distance of the landscape, the weather, and the thickness of the glass, the expanse outside appears in different degrees of distortion. What a passenger sees starts to blur with what she *might* have seen, but cannot confirm, because the moment has already passed. Just as startling, too, is the reflection that can suddenly return, say, when a train enters a tunnel. Such is the uncanny nature of a train window: The viewer is sometimes glimpsed alongside the view, and this is all the more charged when she is a woman. It is a surface that can startle, and that in certain conditions can be read. For those who know how to decipher it, a mark made on a window, like the one Miss Froy traces with her finger, becomes a kind of invisible ink.

Another woman appears in a train window in Chantal Akerman's *News from Home* (1976). Inside a subway car, the interior lights reveal Akerman standing in profile, her shirt-sleeves rolled up. Her arm holds onto a tripod just out of view as she bobs up and down with the rushing train. Another woman, the cinematographer Babette Mangolte, is barely visible from behind the camera. She is dressed in black and covered by a dark velvet hood. All that can be seen of her is the glint of her wristwatch, or some other piece of jewelry.

This is the only time we actually see Akerman in the film. But she speaks throughout, reading letters sent by her mother. Her voice is heard over images of New York City, which was then on the brink of bankruptcy. The city is especially derelict and ragged, its residents sweltering in polyester suits in the summer heat. Five years earlier, in 1971, a twenty-one-year-old Akerman had arrived there after leaving her family without a word. Though she later returned to Brussels, the letters from Natalia Akerman that she reads aloud in *News from Home* date from that earlier period. No wonder her mother is anxious—the flatness of Akerman's delivery cannot conceal her worry—and the long stares of passengers in the subway, most of them men, only intensifies the sense of hostility and threat.

In the film's two other shots taken from a moving subway, the camera is positioned in the middle of the car, facing down the corridor through the open doors onto the adjacent compartment. The train's open windows amplify its rattling, overwhelming Akerman's soft voice, which can only be heard when the train slows or stops. People look at the camera, some furtively, many boldly. It is particularly distressing when the lights, which occasionally flicker out, turn back on and reveal the same stares, from the same men, like a horror film. One of them, dressed in a memorable lime-green ensemble, would be ridiculous were it not for his unbroken stare, which, even as he walks to the next car, he continues to throw back. It is as if these looks could crowd out the mother's words, shaped by the daughter's voice, and sever the tenuous, epistolary connection to home.

This type of gawking is usually discouraged in public life, though, as most women know all too well, it occurs quite frequently. What a woman wears, how she moves, where and how she looks—just about anything can provoke the unwanted gaze of men. The situation of being a woman on a train requires what Lynne Kirby has called a "practical ambivalence."[1] Because trains have been associated with a prevailing masculinity, apparent in the suggestive phallic shape of the train, the commonplace allusion to intercourse in the trope of a train entering a tunnel, the coding of train engineers as male, and the marketing of model trains to boys, women have been more often put at the effect of both men and trains. As with other public spaces, it can be dangerous for a woman to be too friendly or too cold. She can look, but not too much. She must tolerate being looked at, perhaps more than she would like. *News From Home* upends this practical ambivalence by firmly planting the filmmaker, her cinematographer, and their tripod-mounted camera in full view of the male subway riders who feel entitled to stare. In fleeting window reflections, we are reminded of Akerman's presence and steadfastness. The men may look, but the woman endures.

In *Calamity* (1982), about a college dropout who becomes a train driver, Věra Chytilová deliberately makes the filmmaker-passenger visible. The film begins with a shot through a glass door separating a train compartment and its vestibule. The glass creates a composite image, combining a view of both spaces. People on both sides crowd the shot: At the end of the car, someone holds a camera, evidently preparing for a tracking shot, and within the vestibule, held in the camera's shallow focus, a man with a cigarette in hand steps into frame. He lowers his head as though he is waiting for a signal. On the near side of the door, a woman with dark hair, presumably Chytilová, leans out from behind the camera (she stands behind Ivan Slapeta, the cinematographer), and gives the man the sign to enter. We see her in the reflection of the glass. The man stubs out his cigarette, then opens the door and walks through it, joining in the car with the director and cinematographer. The camera loses focus as he approaches, then pulls back, holding him in a tight frame as he peers out a window and smiles at a female passenger standing next to him.

The shot appears to be the footage captured prior to the director's call of "action." Normally such a shot would be edited out of a film; another director, for instance, might begin the film with the opening of the door. But Chytilová's

Brechtian insertion serves a different purpose. By including this earlier moment of waiting along with her own obscured image behind the camera, she indicates that the events of the film, which eventually careen into an avalanche both natural and bureaucratic in nature, are all set in motion by a single woman. Though she is only visible for a moment, there is no doubt that there is, at all times, a woman looking. In film, women are not often prioritized as the ones who do the looking—we need only recall Laura Mulvey's famous assertion that, in the classical cinema, men look, while women are there to be looked at.[2] But these examples remind us that women see far more, and perhaps differently, than we realize. Sometimes it takes a reflection in the glass to notice that there is a woman who has been watching all along.

A woman who vanishes can be just as provocative as one who unexpectedly appears. In Olivier Assayas's *Clouds of Sils Maria* (2014), two women ride a train together through the Swiss Alps. Val (Kristen Stewart) works as the personal assistant to Maria (Juliette Binoche), a successful actress on her way to accept an award on behalf of the reclusive playwright Wilhelm Melchior. When she was eighteen, Maria was cast in Melchior's play *The Maloja Snake*, about a relationship between an older woman and a younger one hired to be her assistant. Now, twenty years later, Maria is conflicted about revisiting the same play, this time in the role of Helena, the older character who is seduced and ultimately destroyed by the younger Sigrid. The dynamic between Val and Maria mirrors that of the characters in the play. Though there is nothing explicitly erotic between them, its possibility remains open as they argue, smoke, and drink—other forms of intimacy. Then there is the shot of Maria who spies Val asleep on her belly, her thong exposed.

The narrative twists and double backs on itself, like the train that winds through narrow alpine passes, during which times Val's phone loses reception. It is also matched by the clouds of the film's title, a reference to the rare and mysterious Maloja Snake, a dense roll of fog that sweeps through the mountains. The distinctions between fictional and real, past and present, are especially blurred when the two women rehearse lines in preparation for Maria's return to the play. Maria protests, disgusted by Helena. She insists that she's nothing like her. Val argues that Helena is just like the reckless Sigrid: They are "two women with the same wound." They are, perhaps, the same woman.

In the play, a distraught Helena commits suicide. This act especially upsets Maria. There, too, Val counters—Helena doesn't necessarily die, she just disappears. This scenario is echoed in the hike that Val and Maria take after they arrive at Melchior's home. On the way to a spot where they can view the Maloja Snake, they bicker, and Val falls behind. Maria climbs the bluff and sees the Snake starting to form in the valley. She turns; Val is not there. Throughout the film the two women have circled each other, traded places, and now, in a repetition of the play they rehearse, one has suddenly disappeared. It is as though she has disembarked from a metaphorical train, which in this film, is the same as a tunnel of fog. Maria is left without the woman who was, in many ways, her younger self. Or maybe she has finally accepted the other woman into, or as, herself? Assayas leaves the question open. Val never returns, and is eventually replaced by a new assistant, with whom Maria maintains a cool distance.

The play is eventually mounted with a brash American actress in the role of Sigrid. On opening night, Maria arrives onstage and walks through a warren of glass cubicle walls built for the play's modern office setting. The camera tracks with her, first viewing her through multiple planes of glass, then shedding these translucent layers until there is nothing between the camera and its view of her. By this point Maria is seated in her chair, unmoving, a cigarette burning in her hand. The camera studies her, but her expression refuses transparency. The lights dim, and a sly smile flickers across her face.

The popularity of the vanishing lady motif dates back to at least the late nineteenth century. Karen Redrobe calls the Vanishing Lady Trick of 1886, a wildly successful stage act performed by magician Buatier DeKolta and his wife Alice, the moment when "vanishing firmly establishes itself as female."[3] Its form appeared in numerous cultural spaces—in many magic films of Georges Méliès, especially *The Vanishing Lady* (*L'Escamotage d'une dame chez Robert-Houdin*) (1896), where a woman turns into a skeleton; Robert W. Paul's *The Vanishing Lady* (1897), which enacts the Pygmalion myth only to have the Galatea figure disappear from the waist up; and in L. Frank Baum's publication *The Art of Decorating Dry Goods Windows and Interiors* (1900), where the author of *The Wizard of Oz* describes a window display called "The Vanishing Lady." To entice the customer, Baum advised, a shop owner could use an illusion popularized by "dime museums and side shows."[4] In the window, they could install a live female model who would periodically disappear and return wearing new garments. Anne Friedberg has argued that the use of the vanishing lady in shop windows allowed stores to maximize "consumer contemplation," holding shoppers' attention with a changing window display without requiring that they enter the store.[5]

Like the magician's stage or the shop display, the train window can frame an image of a woman and offer her up for visual consumption. Her vanishings and apparitions become spectacular feats of showmanship. If the train is in motion, the sense of (consumer) contemplation is enhanced. The train is an enclosed space, and movement aboard is often limited. Passenger mobility is traded for looking: out the window, at a book, or at other passengers. Glass, as Friedberg reminds us, is a material for viewing as well as confinement. For instance, sheet glass was critical to Bentham's design for the panopticon, where "the transparency of glass was utilized for surveillance, while at the same time its solidity as a building material functioned to guarantee confinement."[6] On a train, glass similarly extends the look while constraining the body. People, and women especially, become images: momentarily fixed in place on a pane of glass, like a glass plate in still photography, which is to say a picture, an object.

A picture is how General Khaled (Omar Sharif) first encounters Nawal (Faten Hamama) in *The River of Love* (1960), Ezz El-Dine Zulficar's liberally adapted version of Leo Tolstoy's *Anna Karenina*.[7] Nawal is asleep in her cabin on a train, a book in her lap. The camera pulls back to reveal her duplicate image being surreptitiously sketched by Wasfy, an artist, who peers through her compartment door. "Look," Wasfy exclaims, and he shows his drawing to Khaled, who has been standing in the corridor. Khaled demands to see this sleeping beauty, and the two men stare into her door. Their excited chatter awakens Nawal, but she doesn't let on.

Anna Karenina, of course, is very nearly paradigmatic for the pitfalls of being a woman on a train, as the railroad brings her to ruin. In the novel, Anna's chance encounter with the dashing Count Vronsky occurs with her arrival at the Moscow train station. The moment is marred when a railway worker is crushed under the locomotive's wheels. It is a bad start to what will become a tragic love affair: Anna is trapped in a loveless marriage, with a son, and Vronsky's affections prove capricious. Eventually Anna, alone and forsaken, succumbs to the same fate that she witnessed that day on the platform.

The filmed adaptations of the novel, including *The River of Love*, all introduce Anna with great care. In Julien Duvivier's 1948 version, she is even introduced twice. First, at the start of the film, a snow-covered train flies through the landscape. The camera slowly tracks into a carriage window, which is obscured by billowing steam. Gradually Anna's (Vivian Leigh) face emerges, delicately framed within the frost-deckled glass like a cameo brooch. Then, a similar introduction is repeated for Vronsky. The train has just arrived at the station in Moscow, and Anna peers out the window, searching for her brother. She wipes the glass with a handkerchief, creating a halo of fog. This is how Vronsky sees her from the platform: like a mannequin in a window display.

The perception of people as objects is in some ways an invention of the train. To describe the profound sensorial transformation that occurred with the advent of train travel, Wolfgang Schivelbusch writes: "[S]hot through the landscape . . . [and] thus losing control of one's senses . . . the traveler ceased to be a traveler and became, as noted in a popular metaphor of the century, a mere parcel."[8] People became objects, like the cargo carried in the freight trains that preceded passenger travel, or the packages efficiently transported across Britain in Basil Wright and Harry Watt's *Night Mail* (1936).[9] The situation compounds when women, already considered objects of specular desire, ride trains in film.

Take Greta Garbo's Anna, from Clarence Brown's 1935 version. (Brown, who frequently put trains in his films, also directed *Possessed*, mentioned in this book's introduction.) The train window is the pretext for Vronsky's (Frederic March) first glimpse at Anna. He walks along the platform, looking for his mother in the windows of the arriving train. He finds her, motions for her to meet him, and backtracks to the door. A gust of steam turns the image almost entirely gray, then dissipates. Because we have been following Vronsky, we expect to see the older woman that was just in the window; instead, it is Garbo who appears. Abruptly, the fog returns, then parts again. Anna, unmoving and statuesque, is like a chimera, suddenly visible, and justly as quickly gone. Vronsky stares intensely at her, as if to hold onto her image. This rendering is the closest to the novel, in which a guard leads Vronsky to his mother's compartment, and where, at the door, the fateful first look with Anna is exchanged. But Brown, it seems, could not resist the cinematic insertion of a window, a frame within the frame. (Most faithful but least cinematic is Joe Wright's windowless 2012 *Anna Karenina*, in which the future lovers briefly pass as Anna exits and Vronsky boards the car.)

Garbo's Anna is the most enigmatic because she is the most outwardly composed. After her visit to Moscow, which included another run-in with Vronsky, she departs for St. Petersburg by rail. She tries to stifle the passion the count has aroused in her. Next to her, a woman complains of the cold, and asks if Anna agrees. From beneath her fur blanket, she answers with a polite nod, then looks back at her book. As Tolstoy describes, Anna has difficulty concentrating on her reading; "[s]he had too great a desire to live herself" (Chapter 29). At a stop, as in the novel, she announces she is going out for air, and steps off the train. The snow swirls forcefully, an externalized sign of the turmoil within her. Wandering along the platform, Garbo's Anna breathes a sigh of relief—one of her few unguarded moments. Then the bell calls her back to the train, to her life and duty.

But Vronsky intercepts her again. He has followed her from Moscow and finds her as she boards the train. He declares his love for her, and, overwhelmed, she runs back to her cabin. But she does not sleep like the other passengers around her. Instead, she leans sharply forward, staring out the window, the sun rising over a distant hilltop. What could she be thinking? Garbo's tensed posture suggests what Tolstoy makes explicit: "She did not sleep all night. But in that nervous tension, and in the visions that filled her imagination, there was nothing disagreeable or gloomy: on the contrary there was something blissful, glowing, and exhilarating" (Chapter 30). The scene cuts to the reverse angle, from outside the train, with Anna framed in the window once again, alone in her thoughts. There is no voiceover to speak Tolstoy's words, only the quiet rumble of the train, and the somber choir in the film's score. Garbo sighs, and her eyelids lower. Is there a hint of satisfaction in her expression?

The story of *Anna Karenina* is undeniably tragic, and its lesser adaptations treat its heroine as inseparable from her fate. But even in the most considered versions, there's a tendency to indulge in Anna's suffering, both bodily and emotionally, especially in the scene of her suicide. This is perhaps inevitable. It is demonstrated by the YouTube compilation "Different Versions of Anna Karenina Train Deaths," which replaces the audio from a half dozen film and television adaptations with a bombastic, discordant score, and asks viewers to list their favorite death scenes in the comments.[10] But these, I maintain, are different from the Annas that turn inward while riding the train, the women who think, see, and desire. In the double reflection of Garbo's Anna offered by the train glass, she is both the commodity and the contemplative consumer, both the image and its viewer.

Were I to do a YouTube montage (don't worry, I won't), it would be of women on trains, absorbed in their thoughts. I would retrieve these moments from the most odious and moralizing of films, like Adrian Lyne's *Unfaithful* (2002), a tawdry cousin to Anna Karenina, in which suburban housewife Connie (Diane Lane) ventures to Manhattan to buy birthday party supplies for her son and, during a windstorm, is swept into the arms of the hot, young Frenchman Paul (Olivier Martinez). Their ensuing affair is about as subtle as a stock-porn plot, and its violent end is as punishing as it is predictable (apart from the unexpected use of a snow globe repurposed into a murder weapon). What I remember, however, is Connie's train ride home after their first tryst. Her face is red and her movements are restless. A smile leaks out, then laughter, then she covers her face with her hands, as though hiding her delight. She smooths her hair and sits up. Her hand finds her chest, and she's reminded all over again of the encounter. Lyne intercuts the moment with a flashback of Paul going down on her, though none of that is necessary. In the barely contained excitement Lane expresses, and all that comes with it—terror, regret, and desire for more—she reverses the direction of a century of train erotics. The woman goes from being desired to the one who does the desiring. Never mind that this is a Lyne film, and that the wayward wife will eventually pay for her infidelity. Lane's face, her eyes serenely closed, are enough to forget all that happens afterward.

One of the most remarkable scenes of a woman sitting on a train, and only sitting, comes from *The Flavor of Green Tea over Rice* (Yasujirō Ozu, 1952). Before she boards the train, the haughty Taeko (Michiyo Kogure), whom I think Ozu unduly maligns, had been squabbling with her husband Mokichi (Shin Saburi). She picked a fight with him over the way he was slurping his bowl of rice. No doubt there was an undercurrent of dissatisfaction as happens in many marriages. Her husband plays innocent, professing an enjoyment of "intimate and primitive things, without modesty or constraints," simple pleasures like cheap cigarettes and riding third class on the train. What is a wife supposed to do with that? Admit that she likes fussy things? Instead, Taeko, undoubtedly the smarter of the two, declares, "I'll ride trains as I like." In the next scene, she has set out on a long-distance voyage, first class of course. She stares ahead of her, not seeing the flower in the vase, or the tracks that shrink behind her in the otherwise empty caboose. For nearly two minutes, we watch her sit. Over the PA, the train conductor announces upcoming stops: Hamamatsu, Nagoya, Kyoto, Osaka. Taeko remains unmoved. Sullen, yes, and perhaps a little sad. But she has at least achieved a few hours "without modesty or constraints," indulging in feelings that belong to no one but her.

Juho Kuosmanen's *Compartment No. 6* (2021) offers another portrait of a solitary woman on a train. Outwardly, the overnight train that travels from Moscow to the Arctic outpost Murmansk is only a means of transporting Laura (Seidi Haarla), a Finnish archaeology student, to the prehistoric petroglyphs that were discovered there in 1997. But Laura's excitement extends beyond the academic. This was to have been a romantic getaway with Irina, a pretentious literature professor whom we meet surrounded by her equally insufferable friends. Not quite realizing the shallowness of Irina's

attachment, Laura departs for the ancient rock carvings alone. Along the way, she is comforted by footage she reviews in her camcorder—"my whole Moscow," she calls it—while generally avoiding her crude compartment-mate Lyokha (Yura Borisov), a Russian miner. She also uses the camera to film out the window, not the passing landscape, but the glass itself, where the dust on its surface is transformed into an array of cascading lights. It's a subtle but significant difference in perspective.

At this stage in the journey, Laura is afraid or perhaps unwilling to see the truth about her relationship. Later, another passenger steals her camera. Laura is bereft, but the misfortune allows her to open up to Lyokha, with whom she develops a tender and uncategorizable bond. By the time she arrives in Murmansk, she has changed. On the phone, Irina sounds as distant as ever. This is also true for Laura. "Everything seems to be too far away," she says. From the narrow confines of the train, whose every lurch is felt, thanks to Kuosmanen's insistence on shooting on a moving Soviet-era train, to the broad, flat rocks of the petroglyphs on the edge of the White Sea, and with Lyokha beside her, Laura is finding her way between too close and too far, between one side of the glass and the other.

This is no small distance. King Vidor's *Stella Dallas* (1937) contains one of the most painful scenes of separation by a window. In that film, famously, Barbara Stanwyck's Stella stands outside a rain-streaked window watching her daughter's wedding. Lolly (Anne Shirley), Stella's affectionate nickname for Laurel, doesn't know her mother is there. There's a lot that Lolly doesn't know about Stella, including the sacrifices she made so that her daughter could enjoy a privileged life that was denied to her. But the scene that destroys me is when Lolly departs for New York to live with her father and his new, patrician family. Only Stella knows it's the last time her daughter will ever see her. From the platform, she grasps Lolly's hand through the open window of the train. She smiles tearfully, barely concealing her sorrow, but firm in her conviction that removing herself is necessary to securing her daughter's happiness. She believes this, but she also holds on until, finally, the train rips them apart.

Itinerary

London to Venice

Midway through Joanna Hogg's *The Souvenir* (2019), Julie (Honor Swinton Byrne) and Anthony (Tom Burke) take a train to Venice. It is also midway in their troubled relationship. Julie, an aspiring filmmaker, is young and tentative. She is drawn to the debonair Anthony, who wears pinstripes and velvet loafers, knows about opera, and regularly takes tea at Harrods. At the Wallace Collection, Anthony brings Julie to see Jean-Honoré Fragonard's *The Souvenir*, which depicts Jean-Jacques Rousseau's heroine Julie as she carves the initials of her beloved's name into a tree. Our Julie finds her expression sad. Anthony says she looks "determined . . . and very much in love." On this last point they agree.

Anthony claims to work for the foreign office. He says this in a fairly unconvincing way, but not knowing about Anthony's past is what appeals to Julie. While reading aloud a passage about Venice from E. Temple Thurston's *The City of Beautiful Nonsense*, she pauses to study two photos of Anthony tucked into the back of the book. In one he is in a tuxedo. "I like this," she says. In the other, he wears a turban and a beard. "Where

was this taken?" she asks. "Afghanistan. '73," he replies, stubbing out his cigarette.

They board the luxurious Venice Simplon Orient Express. In their private car, cloaked in wood paneling and burgundy drapes, Anthony sings off-key, but with no less confidence. Julie smiles. Everything is splendid on the train. Anthony is in a suit; no surprise there. But Julie, who normally wears oversized oxford shirts, sports a tailored gray suit reminiscent of Kim Novak's ensemble in Alfred Hitchcock's *Vertigo* (1958). The fabric puckers a little as she slouches, her hands folded in her lap. Above them are matching monogrammed suitcases. On the table between them, a bottle of champagne is nestled in a bucket of ice. For now, everything is good.

Terrible things have happened and there is more to come. In the scene just prior, Julie's Knightsbridge flat had been robbed, her jewelry and film equipment taken. The couple embraced when they found their ransacked home. They decided to not cancel their trip. After their train journey, when they arrive at their large, dark apartment in Venice, Julie tips the porter. Though by now she is accustomed to footing the bill, she buries her head in her hands. "Please tell me what I've done," Anthony pleads. She perhaps suspects, and only later confirms, that Anthony had been the one to break in, because he needed to buy heroin, to feed the addiction that would eventually take his life.

But on the train, the trees in the window are a blur, London is far away, and they are both happy. A shot of Venice appears, reflected upside down in dark water. The train is a world of fantasy, like the movies. Julie's choice of clothing makes that clear. Though the high-collar buttoning wouldn't meet Scotty's specifications in *Vertigo*—imagine Jimmy Stewart vigorously shaking his head, sputtering "that's not it, nothing like it!"—here it is exactly right. This is as much Julie's fantasy as it is Anthony's; it is her fantasy of *him*. Unlike Judy (Novak), who squirms and pulls away from Scotty, Julie delights in her fitting. Julie and Anthony are playing characters they both approve of. This too is a form of intimacy. At film school, an instructor asks Julie: "What makes you want to leave your own experience so radically and enter into this very different world?" He is speaking of her plan to film a domestic drama in Sunderland, a working-class city of shipyards far removed from Julie's posh upbringing. But the question equally applies aboard the luxury train: Why entertain such beautiful nonsense? Because it is beautiful, because it is nonsensical, because she is in love.

In *Vertigo*, the dresses are modeled by shop assistants in a department store. Scotty looks only at the clothes; Judy, flustered, is desperate to leave. The opposite is the case in Max Ophuls's *Letter from an Unknown Woman* (1948). There the clothes in the shop where Lisa (Joan Fontaine) works are a pretense for the models to walk and turn about. The unspoken rule is that shopgirls accept dates from interested clients. Demure Lisa is the only one who refuses—as the shopkeeper explains to a rebuffed customer, she alone goes straight home after work. That is until the pianist Stefan Brand (Louis Jourdan) comes in. He is also uninterested in dresses. He has tracked Lisa down after an impromptu affair that took them first to a lavish restaurant then to a winter carnival. In the shop, he asks her to see him off at the train station before he departs. She obliges. But at the station the dashing Stefan is surrounded by women clamoring for his attention. He pulls away to find Lisa, who smiles bashfully at him. "I still know so little about you," he says. The women call for him, and he returns to them. Lisa's face falls. The spell is broken. As we will later learn, and as Lisa already knows, he will callously forget her. Like the woman in the Fragonard painting, she is sad, determined, and very much in love.

When was the spell most potent? At the carnival, Lisa and Stefan step into a train carriage whose window opens onto a moving diorama. "We're in Venice!" she exclaims delightedly. Stefan steps out to request a new destination: Switzerland, which a man lowers like the backdrop to an opera, then steadily pedals a modified bicycle to advance the view. Within the cabin enclosure, Lisa talks about her father, whose friend worked in a travel bureau, and who allowed her to visit far-flung destinations by pouring over their brochures. Stefan listens, rapt. She is enchanting. He wants to know more about her, though it isn't clear that he has even asked her name.

Soon, they have run out of countries to visit. "Then we'll begin all over again!" Stefan declares. "We'll revisit the scenes of our youth." For a moment, the entire world is available to them. All the time they might have enjoyed together seems within their grasp now, in the imagined circuit of this fake train. It is a most romantic loop.

"We'll revisit the scenes of our youth." These words could describe the autobiographical nature of *The Souvenir* and its follow-up *The Souvenir Part II* (2021), in which Hogg restaged her experiences as a young filmmaker, down to the London flat she meticulously reconstructed on a soundstage. They also describe Lisa's narration, which forms the structure of the film, a series of recollections recorded in a letter. Already in this scene, narrated by Lisa and played out in the film, the diorama ride is like a memory. This fantastical train moves backward into a past that is warm and glowing because it is a moment they are together. Venice, too, holds special meaning for Ophuls. At the conclusion of *The Company's in Love* (1932), studio executive Loring consoles the distressed would-be actress Gretl by pulling from his pocket two train tickets. The film cuts to a close-up showing the destination "Venedig": a direction, an idea, a fantasy.

Most passengers, of course, do not ride trains this way. Trains run along fixed routes, certain in their destinations. There is no mystery about where they end up. In another Ophuls film, *From Mayerling to Sarajevo* (1940), about the love affair between Archduke Franz Ferdinand (John Lodge) and the Countess Sophie Chotek (Edwige Feuillère), the pair ride a fateful train to Sarajevo. We know all too well the world-historical shift that will happen next. But in this lavish compartment, history and fantasy share the same track. Franz and Sophie giggle and drink; they act like kids. "No more traveling without your wife!" she scolds him from atop his lap. There's a lightness between them that isn't present at any other moment in the film, not even during their flirtatious first encounter. As the end draws near, the train offers a kind of gift: an expanse opened as the seconds wind down.

2

Ends of the Line

The ideology of the train is one of smoothness. Trains glide along their rails, and in coordinated synchronization along an efficient network. There are no obstacles, no delays, no surprises. They make up the arterial system of capital, shuttling parcels and people in line and on time, like a mechanized heartbeat. This ideology of smoothness is at once natural and abstract, both a basic law of physics and its ideal. Wolfgang Schivelbusch cites Isaac Newton in his account of a "perfect road": "smooth, level, hard and straight."[1] The train, in its highest as well as its inevitable form, runs along a similarly frictionless path.

Because of this perceived smoothness, the train has been an indelible feature of fascist regimes. In Greta Gerwig's *Barbie* (2023), a cynical teenager accuses the title character of being a fascist, and Barbie (Margot Robbie) weeps in bewildered protest: "I don't control the railways or the flow of commerce!" The train, and the immense Nazi infrastructure it supported, is central to Claude Lanzmann's *Shoah* (1985), a documentary without peer, in large part because of Lanzmann's willingness to delve into the minutiae of a genocide, including locomotive conductors, railway workers, bureaucrats, survivors, and witnesses who rode, watched, or did their best to ignore the trains that delivered millions to their deaths. Eschewing archival footage, Lanzmann films in the present to evoke a past that was still palpable. Much of the film takes place along the routes that once led to Chelmno, Treblinka, Sobibor, Auschwitz, and Birkenau, their carriages arriving full and leaving empty. Some tracks are covered in grass; some sections are still in use. In the film's most harrowing shot, a grizzled driver leans out the window of a train arriving at Treblinka. The train slows and he squints. He does not speak, and he is not interviewed elsewhere in the film. After the train stops, he draws his finger across his neck. This same gesture appears in Richard Glazar's recollection, when, as a child riding aboard a train carrying Czech Jews to Treblinka, he saw it made by a Polish bystander. The gesture is chilling, not least for its ambiguity. Is it a warning? A threat? And what are we to make of its survival from a horrific past into a still-unsettled present? Lanzmann ends his film with another train, likely the same as one from an earlier shot, also at Treblinka. Its direction, toward arrival or from departure, is hard to determine. The train enters the frame. Its headlights glow in the dusk. The film cuts before the train exits the frame, though the sound continues into the end credits. It is a train that does not cease.

Lynne Kirby has argued that the train "tried to make the world readable": bumps flattened, curves straightened, and passengers, from the metropole to the periphery, brought into obedient order. The apparent triumph of smoothness is evident in the vast networks of railways built in the nineteenth and early twentieth centuries, which left little of the world untouched. At the same time, this prevailing idea of the train has required the constant invocation of its unstable other. In order for its modernization story to have purchase, so too did its opponent have to be formidable. Attending each instance of railroad boosterism, then, has been the shadow of disorder.

This is also the story of cinema: A fundamentally heterogeneous medium that learned to produce an illusion of continuity through subtle cinematographic and editing cues. Kirby writes that in both cinema and the train, "each has historically represented its own instability as the opposite—a 'smooth ride' on a constantly shifting vehicle—by integrating the modern, primarily urban subject into a larger, mechanically defined world."[2] For every feat of "integration, of linkage, of coherence" achieved by the architects of railway systems, these marvels turned on the threat of the opposite: disintegration, breakdown, illogic. Train films, especially those that describe the historical beginnings and ends of the railroad, are especially adept at exploiting these contradictions.

Take the mechanical reality of trains. Against their frictionless ideal, trains are subject to "internal contradictions . . . irregularities . . . jolts."[3] They can and do break down. (Riders of New York City's MTA subway system, especially, are intimately familiar with the frequency of train disruptions.) But in film, this is rarely the result of mechanical failure. The reasons are more often spectacular: a criminal hijacking (*The Taking of Pelham 1 2 3*, 1974, along with its 2009 remake); an avalanche (*Calamity*, 1982); an incapacitated driver (*Runaway Train*, 1985); revenge-motivated sabotage (*The Burning*

Train, 1980); politically motivated sabotage (*V for Vendetta*, 2005); historically politically motivated sabotage (*The Train*, 1964); the deliberate destruction of a passenger train carrying a highly infectious virus (*The Cassandra Crossing*, 1976); the attempted murder of a teenage spy (*The Commuter*, 2018); a terrorist attack that can only be stopped retroactively by a time-traveling soldier (*Source Code*, 2011); a wreck indirectly caused by zombies (*Train to Busan*, 2016); and various superhero antics (*The Incredibles* [2004], *Shang-Chi and the Legend of the Ten Rings* [2021], many Spiderman films). Even when trains are seen to labor, they are fantastical creations, like the locomotive that wheezes positive affirmations to itself in *Dumbo* (1941).

Bong Joon-Ho's *Snowpiercer* (2013) is the rare train film whose culminating disaster is a result of both mechanical failure and spectacular contrivance. This dystopian sci-fi thriller takes place in a near future where most life on Earth has been frozen out of existence. The exception is a high-speed train that circumnavigates the globe. This "rattling ark" is entirely self-sufficient, and a group of schoolchildren aboard the wealthier section of the train sing a hymn to its "eternal engine." But for it to keep running, a strict order must be maintained, including a social hierarchy organized by carriage position. Outwardly the film is about a rebellion of the lowest ranks against their authoritarian captors, but its real opponents are the forces of control and contingency. Those at the front of the train fetishize their "closed ecological system," down to a calendar-regulated serving of sushi, while the denizens of the "Curtis Revolution," named for their dogged leader (Chris Evans), smash their way forward from the tail. But this violent convulsion turns out to be part of the calculation too: As Wilford (Ed Harris), the train's designer, explains, it is a ruthless but effective form of population control.

Strangely, though the film pays significant attention to the train's engine, namely who controls it, its mechanical durability is not in question. On a couple of occasions, passengers brace for the impact of the train smashing through ice and snow that naturally accrue on the tracks. No one seems worried that the train might derail, despite its breakneck speed. In fact, this is how the water system maintains its supply, by collecting snow to later melt. For this reason, *Snowpiercer* is a popular topic of conversation among train enthusiasts on the r/trains subreddit, who enjoy griping about its implausible engineering. TransTrainNerd2816 remarks, "i had to explan the railways are very high maintenance and must have track and locomotives taken out of service regularly espcialley with steam traction [*sic*]."[4] OutlyingPlasma is more direct: "Does no one realize how much work goes into maintaining tracks yet somehow this one train can just keep circulating a frozen uninhabited wasteland for generations?" And with utter seriousness, InsideSpeed8785 muses, "I would want a very wide guage for the end of the world [*sic*]."[5]

This is more than just unrealistic representation, or the sport of (train) spotting continuity errors. The irony of *Snowpiercer* is that its interest in engine maintenance, including the manual labor required to keep it running, turns against its own fantastical conceit. When characters utter lines like "we control the engine, we control the world," or when we are shown the train hurtling into a wall of ice, it means that issues of mechanical maintenance are, in fact, central to the narrative. It's impossible not to notice when something—Curtis's forearm instead of the proverbial wrench—is quite literally thrown into the gears. One needn't be an ardent train enthusiast to notice the artificial smoothness by which this train magically runs.

In films about the history of the railroad, even the most heroic narratives invoke a sense of disorder, contingency, and a future that might have turned out otherwise. Its founding, raised to the status of legend, is told in John Ford's *The Iron Horse* (1924), about the completion of the transcontinental railway in the United States. Ford's westerns, of course, are well known for their mythologizations (and counter-mythologizations) of the American frontier. The arrival of the train often signals the end of an untrammeled way of life. With *The Man Who Shot Liberty Valence* (1962) for example, the sound of a train can be heard at the exact moment when Tom Doniphon (John Wayne) sets fire to the home he was building for his sweetheart Hallie. With this act of destruction, he erases his presence from the land, and makes way for the train, which brings with it the rule of law, democratic institutions, and Tom's romantic rival, the East Coast lawyer Rance Stoddard (Jimmy Stewart). As with many westerns, the arrival of the train spells the closing of the frontier, and with it, the end of its way of life. Ford approached this with ambivalence and a sense of inevitability.

With the earlier *The Iron Horse*, Ford focuses on the railroad's role in shaping the nation. Abraham Lincoln, to whom the film is dedicated, is central to this vision. Called "the great rail-splitter president" in an intertitle, he meets with Congress to approve the construction of the transnational railroad. Against a naysayer who insists, I think rather reasonably, that the Civil War effort should come before this "engineering folly," Lincoln gravely intones that "we will have fought in vain" if they do not first secure a country unified by rail and willpower.

Railroad construction proceeds through wartime strife as well as unceded Indigenous territory. The film's title comes from the supposed Native American name for the train, an undefeatable "iron horse" that contributed to the near-total eradication of Native life in the country. Here, they are called "defiant" in an intertitle, and they attack the railroad builders in an ambush. This, however, only slows construction. The term "iron horse," meanwhile, was domesticated to the cutesy "ferroequinologist," another name for a train hobbyist.

The Central Pacific, which stretches eastward from Sacramento, and the Union Pacific, which runs westward from Omaha, are joined when Leland Stanford hammers in the famed Golden Spike at Promontory Summit in Utah Territory, an event which took place on May 10, 1869. Davy (George O'Brien), a Lincoln true believer, has been waiting for this moment his entire life. Davy is perhaps the only individual to work both ends of the railway. He is strapping and decent, unlike the corrupt landowner Deroux, who is interested only in maximizing payouts to himself. Davy's story mirrors the fate of the transcontinental railroad. Both are stymied by various opponents—greed and graft, snow and violence—but they are destined to emerge triumphant. Lincoln's disembodied head, which in an early scene glows like that of a saint, all but ordains this. Davy even manages to win the girl, though it takes a fairly tortured bit of plot maneuvering for this to occur. As the last stretch of track is laid, he grabs Miriam, the daughter of a railway owner, and declares, "when they drive the golden spike we'll belong to each side . . . and each other."

Putting aside the film's narrative clumsiness, Ford went to extraordinary lengths to achieve its sense of realism. All the track that is laid, every tree felled, all the snow shoveled, was actually accomplished for the film—over a mile and a half of track. The entire cast and crew, some three hundred people in total, lived aboard twenty sleeper cars parked in Dodge, Nevada, thirty-five miles outside of Reno. The trains were normally used by a circus, and designed for fairer weather than the wintertime shoot; the shivers we see are real, and one crew member, the dining car steward, ultimately succumbed to the cold.

Midway through the film, there is a lengthy montage of the construction of the railroad. We have departed the story of Davy, and now watch teams of men at work: They cut down trees, hammer in spikes, sing work songs, and cluster around a locomotive to inch it up a steep grade. "There is no white labor—it is necessary to bring in Chinese for the task" reads a title card. Among the coolies pictured in this segment—many of whom were actually members of the Paiute tribe who lived on the Pyramid Lake Paiute Tribe Reservation—are several old Chinese men smoking pipes while on break. Their deep wrinkles are visible in arresting medium close-up. Both details are unusual. Aren't they far too old to be doing such backbreaking work? And why do they get a framing otherwise reserved for the film's principal actors?

For reasons unknown, Ford took pains to include these laborers, who, decades earlier, had themselves worked on the railroad. Clearly, these faces signal a desire for authenticity, to bring in people who had direct connection to the historical story he wished to tell. But by that same token, they interrupt the film, being so unlike the named characters as well as the

other actors who play railway workers. The other coolies appear only in wide shots, identified not by their faces but by backs hunched in work, their supposed Chineseness indicated by the straw hats they wear.

There is no ambiguity about *these* men, however. With the sun baked into their skin, they certainly look like they worked the railroad. Later in the film, in a refrain of the earlier work sequence, another group of laborers toil on the railroad. Once again, there are old Chinese men. One looks back at the camera as he wields a hammer. The workers around him keep their heads down. He shoots what I'm tempted to call a knowing glance. There's a hint of a smile. Is he . . . having fun?

This is the moment, for me, in which *The Iron Horse* undoes its own premise. It is the height of the film's realism—the authenticating presence of the Chinese railway worker. But his grin exceeds this function. It seems to say: Look at all we're doing to recreate events from the past, all these people, all this effort. *Isn't it so funny?* In the midst of a movie that stages the joining of the transcontinental railroad as the result of inevitable and even divine force, this uncredited man's smile interrupts that history's momentum. It reminds me of the smile that Allakariallak flashes in Robert Flaherty's *Nanook of the North* (1922), which creates the possibility of the actor's own amusement, his refusal to be a mere prop or set piece, his own attitude toward the camera. As Fatimah Tobing Rony has said of that early ethnographic film, "from the Inuit point of view he may be seen as laughing at the camera."[6] A couple of years later, in rural Nevada, another smile would effectively arrest time.

By the time *The Iron Horse* was released, the American railroad had already reached its peak. In 1916, over 254,000 miles of track were in use. Its subsequent decline was accelerated in the coming decades by the boom in highway, waterway, and air commerce, and by the 1970s the industry was nearing ruin.[7] A combination of deregulation and privatization revitalized freight services somewhat, but this came at the cost of worker protections, safety, and maintenance. Today, only 140,000 miles of track are still functional.[8]

Tony Scott's thriller *Unstoppable* (2010), based on the runaway CSX 8888 that briefly terrorized north central Ohio in 2001, takes place in this long twilight of the railroad. Most of the action concerns the speeding locomotive, and various efforts to stop it, before it crashes into the densely populated town of Stanton, Pennsylvania. Less attention is given to how the train got away in the first place. Yardmaster Connie Hooper

(Rosario Dawson) calls it "a combination of human error and bad luck." The face of this is hapless Dewey, who, in a series of easily preventable missteps, unknowingly engaged the throttle when he decided to hop out of the engine to adjust a track. The "coaster," which includes thirty-nine cars carrying hazardous chemicals, accelerates to top speed.

Connie's assessment isn't entirely correct. Systemic neglect is what has led to this colossal failure, a result of corporate cost cutting, longer work hours, fewer safety checks, and the forced retirement of veteran workers like Frank Barnes (Denzel Washington) in favor of cheaper "yellow-vest rookies" like baby-faced Will (Chris Pine). Both men are "married to the railroad": loners, maladjusted husbands and fathers, and, in other words, the classic heroes of westerns.[9] The blame might be placed on the film's most identifiable villain, Oscar Galvin, the vice president of train operations, and Connie's boss. Galvin is easy to hate. He's a corporate hack who refuses to derail the train in an area where it's safe to do so, because he thinks it will cost too much in terms of "property and personnel." His own plan of dropping an engineer aboard the train via helicopter results, unsurprisingly, in the man's death, but even then he doesn't abandon his hubris. When Frank, who is riding with Will aboard a separate locomotive, offers a risky but heroic intervention, Galvin threatens to fire him. "You already have," Frank retorts, explaining that he received his ninety-day notice seventy-two days prior. Galvin scoffs over the two-way radio. "You're going to risk your life for us with three weeks left?" Frank responds with a curt steeliness only Denzel can pull off: "Not for you."

Of course, Frank and Will persevere, reversing Connie's formulation into one of "human competence and good luck."

A montage sequence at the end confirms the distribution of justice: Frank's job is restored, Will reunites with his estranged family, Connie is installed in Galvin's now vacant position, and Dewey takes a job flipping burgers. But what the film leaves unspoken is a still broken railway system. Thirteen years later, in 2023, an even longer train—fifty-three cars—carrying toxic cargo derailed in East Palestine, Ohio, releasing a gigantic plume of vinyl chloride into the air. The site of the disaster was not far from the locations that appear in Noah Baumbach's *White Noise* (2022), a film whose centerpiece is a train accident that releases a dangerous chemical substance into the air. Trains and movies collide once again.

When a railway is first constructed, its opening prompts fanfare. (I wonder if ceremonial golden spikes are actually functional, or if they are removed later on.) But its subsequent operation receives less attention, and quieter still is its slow decline, the cars taken out of service, the workers that retire without being replaced, and the tracks that gradually turn to grass. It is true that new lines and services continue to be built today, like high-speed rails and luxury locomotives. But the vast majority of railroad transportation relies on aging and reduced infrastructure, a shadow of the nineteenth- and early twentieth-century ambitions that propelled its construction.

Martin Dicicco's *All That Passes by Through a Window That Doesn't Open* (2017) takes place in the juncture between a dilapidated past and the vision of a modern future. It is a wide space. In the film's first part, a team of workers lay down track for the Baku-Tbilisi-Kars Railway, a new route that connects Azerbaijan, Georgia, and Turkey. The men have not been paid for three months, but they keep working. Alone on a vast plain, they talk about the money that is promised to them, never daring to wonder what will happen if it does not come. Meanwhile, in the second part, Hagop, a brakeman, idles at a mostly abandoned station in Armenia. He watches a television program about the new route. "They ignore the existing railway, and just make a new one," he explains to the camera. The new line will not pass through Armenia, whose border is closed because of an ongoing conflict with Azerbaijan. There is the sense Hagop already knows that his station will not reopen, but he is reluctant to leave. Throwing up his hands, he and the small group gathered at the station declare that it is time to drink. One man, unbuttoning his uniform, coos into a phone: "Come to me, my dear, and the hours will seem like minutes." But the reality of time is different. The future barrels ahead and the past lurches behind. In the middle lies the present, which a title in the film's third part describes as a view of a passing landscape seen through a train window. There are trees and dusk, and the hint of a mountain. It is impossible to identify where we are. The present, the film suggests, is a murky expanse, too far from both origin and destination to clearly discern.

Sompot Chidgasornpongse's *Railway Sleepers* (2016), which spans the entire history of the railroad in Thailand, offers a different view of the life of a railroad. It begins with a lengthy quotation from King Chulalongkorn (Rama V)'s April 11, 1893 address at the opening of what would become the State Railway of Thailand (SRT). The decision to build a national railroad helped to secure Thailand's ability to fend off European nations that had already made colonial incursions elsewhere in Southeast Asia. After the king's lofty speech, the film's first train departs. We are on a jungle route sometime between 2008 and 2016, the years that Chidgasornpongse rode every section of the SRT. Over the course of the film, two days and two nights will pass, and with them, we will see riders of every imaginable variety.

Few films give such a vivid feeling of being on a train. Perhaps it is the sound of the wheels, which are especially loud in the vestibules, and audible through the open windows, as most cars along these routes lack air-conditioning. There's a liveliness among the passengers, from the children who hop up and down in their seats, to the vendors who roam the crowded aisles selling fermented pork and Pepsi, to even the sleepers of the film's title, many of whom have found inventive positions in which to doze. Chidgasornpongse films each person with a rare and gentle curiosity. There is the sense that this train is for them, that it exists to move passengers from place to place, for young people to joke, and others to drunkenly sing, and still others to shake their heads in consternation. Hardly anyone looks at a phone, in part because of the pre-smartphone era in which the film was shot, but also, I like to think, because the train offers so much to see and do: a woman selling astrology pamphlets with guaranteed 80 percent accuracy, a boy who writes in his journal about the banana trees he saw before the train entered a tunnel, a dragonfly perched against the window. Most of the cars are decades old, except for the fluorescent-lit berths of the first-class cabins. These rails are worn and frequently traveled. "This grand aspiration has finally come to fruition," King Chulalongkorn declares, and Chidgasornpongse shows what that really means, a century later. It may be less grandiose than the king imagined, but it more than services the country and its people.

The end of the line: This is where Sergei Dvortsevoy's documentary *Bread Day* (1998) begins. Every Tuesday, a rickety wagon carrying the week's delivery of bread is unhitched from an engine along a forked track, and a group of elderly people push it the rest of the way to their village. They are stymied by snow and three unhelpful, yipping dogs. The cursing begins almost immediately. For hours they snipe at each other, an interval suggested by a momentary cut to black, and a return to a later but very similar stretch of the long journey. Once they are back at Township 3 of Zhikharevo, a sparsely populated worker settlement that an early title card tells us is about eighty kilometers from St. Petersburg, they slide open the door to reveal only a few large trays of loaves, many of which, frankly, look burnt. A trio of women in headscarves and thick coats carry the bread into a shed, where they sort and bundle it. "My hands are frozen," one complains. They waddle through the snow to the local store, which is more like a set in a Beckett play: a single counter, a lightbulb on a string, a door. Meanwhile, the animals seem to sense the commotion. A mother dog snarls at her puppies who greedily clamor for milk. Goats pace on the porch.

The drama of *Bread Day* intensifies in its simplicity. Villagers push a wagon, distribute its bread, then return the cart to its original place. In wide and extended takes, Dvortsevoy captures a system that works, but only barely. The pensioners' advanced age, along with the shoddy state of the train, all point to the unspoken question of how much longer this can last. What happens when the snow is too deep, the wagon breaks down, or the residents become too frail to bring in the bread?

If this is a village approaching its end, it is not succumbing quietly. The grousing ticks up as Tamarka, the sole shopkeeper, begins selling bread. The handful of customers inside immediately start arguing with her. She fires back with surprising force. "Why won't you buy the eggs?" she harangues a man who has just purchased six loaves of bread. "My old rooster lays two eggs and a shot of vodka," he retorts. But he doesn't leave, and instead demands even more bread. The women behind him wait silently; they will soon have their turn to exercise their taunts. "This isn't a town, so there's no bakery, and no transport," Tamarka protests. "You only work one day a week!" yells Nina, an old woman in a red cap.

Things go from bad to worse when the store runs out of bread. This week there is not enough to go around. Other times, when the pensioners' checks don't arrive, the bread is left unsold. Old Volodya, who previously helped unload the cart, is particularly bellicose. Tamarka accuses him of being drunk—he certainly seems it—and tells him to get out of the store. Like the other customers, he doesn't budge. It is as if, instead of bread, these pensioners live off the insults they hurl at each other.

Volodya demands to know whether his wife had settled their account. What he is saying seems to matter less than his insistence to be heard. Tamarka pointedly ignores him, and he wanders outside. A long period of quiet follows with the camera trained on the scuffed floor, as if Dvortsevoy had forgotten to turn it off. The relative calm is interrupted by a goat that steps into the store. Tamarka is too busy muttering to herself to notice it at first. When she does, she rails against "old crows" who are too permissive with their animals, and she swats the goat out with a stick. But the night is not yet over. "Tamarka!" Volodya has reappeared, and he starts to sing (drunkenly): "What has been, has been. The war swept it away. Look for a sweetheart and find what you may." Finally the bread seller has had enough, and she shoves him out the door. A moment later he stumbles back in and declares, amid a stream of obscenities, "you're not getting rid of me!"

It is possible to view *Bread Day* as one of Dvortsevoy's documentaries about people left behind after the end of the Soviet Union. The filmmaker himself evidently abandoned documentary for fiction filmmaking when he realized that his growing success was inversely correlated with the misery of his subjects. However, I find myself marveling at the vigor with which these pensioners bicker. In the midst of their hardships—the heavy cart, the buildings with no evident heating, and a state that has mostly failed them—they summon remarkable energy and creativity, albeit of a morbid sort, in the attacks they lavish upon each other. I can only speculate as to where this vitality comes from, but what impresses me most is its unyielding intensity. It circulates among the group like a life-giving hot potato of insults.

There is a Sisyphean undertone to the ritual of the bread delivery. But the film inverts the myth of the king condemned in the afterlife to forever push a stone up a hill. Presumably, these pensioners have lived their entire lives completing repetitive and arduous tasks like this one. But as the state—Sisyphus's stone, the hill, the structure of the punishment—erodes around them, *they* are the ones who remain, grumbling into eternity.

The lives of railway workers and their trains are intertwined in Claire Denis's *35 Shots of Rum* (2008). Lionel (Alex Descas) works on the RER, a network of trains that connect Paris to its outer periphery. He moves unhurriedly through his routine: long, isolated hours in the cab, where daylight slips into evening. After he returns home from work, his daughter Joséphine (Mati Diop) has dinner waiting for the two of them. They eat greedily, with few words exchanged between them. They are comfortable and close. Such a life could go on a long time, as it probably already has. But for Lionel's coworker René (Julieth Mars-Toussaint), the familiar rhythms of the RER are all he has. On his last day on the job, he and Lionel linger in the locker room. René clears out the contents of his locker, including, taped to the door, a picture of a man spinning dozens

of plates on tall sticks. Lionel sees his friend's eyes welling up with tears. They embrace. "You can't fall apart now, not in front of everyone," Lionel tells him gently.

Later that evening, the mood is buoyant at René's retirement party. Coworkers bestow him with gifts, including a large wooden carving and an iPod. They encourage a reluctant René to speak. "I've waited so long for this," he manages. "It's a deliverance." The note of ambivalence in his voice is lost on a room full of laughter and merriment. He starts to choke up again, but shakes it off to toast with his friends.

There are twenty-nine spinning plates in René's picture. Maybe the number is unimportant, and what matters instead is the symbolism of dozens of fragile things held up in the air with great effort. Each time René tears up or changes the subject, I imagine one falls to the ground. Every long, sad look he gives to Lionel, another plate. And when René takes his own life, his body fallen on the tracks at the terminus of Lionel's line, all of them are lying shattered on the floor. In that wrenching scene, Lionel pulls the brakes early because he sees a foreboding shape ahead of the train. It is dark in the tunnel, but he already seems to know what is there. Denis cuts back to the passengers aboard the train, unaware of what their driver has seen. They hear his voice over the intercom: "Service is interrupted due to a technical incident."

The filmmaker Alice Diop has said of *35 Shots of Rum*:

> In the very opening of *35 Shots of Rum*, the first sequence, I started crying: because all of a sudden I saw this magnificent image of this train, the RER B, making a journey that I have taken all my life, and I discovered the world of my childhood transformed into something sublime by this extremely sensitive camera. It was like I suddenly saw the "non-place" I had grown up in more clearly. And I realized that here, too, there could be cinema, and that it is just as political to film these non-places in a cinematographic way as it is to make a political speech around the question of the center and the periphery.[10]

This non-place becomes the terrain for her documentary *Nous* (2020). The train that forms the geographic skeleton for the observational study is itself only visible between scenes, as b-roll (or, if one prefers, RER B-roll). Along this line, Diop visits individuals who are much like Lionel, René, and the predominantly immigrant and working-class people who ride and work the trains in *35 Shots of Rum*. These are Diop's friends and neighbors, and, in one case, her own family. She follows her sister Ndeye Sighane Diop, a caregiver who travels to her patients' homes to administer their medicine. They are all elderly, and most live alone. Ndeye has a warm demeanor and an easy laugh, and her immense capacity to listen is belied only by the car rides between homes, where she grips the steering wheel and says nothing.

The stories that Ndeye's patients tell hint at the richness of their lives, as well as their proximity to despair. One recounts how she met her husband after he had rescued her from a suicide attempt. Another laments his loneliness following the recent death of his wife, but he admits that he refuses to socialize with others his age. In *Nous*, as with *35 Shots of Rum*, hardship accrues over time. In one scene, a mechanic working in an outdoor parking lot receives a call from his mother in Mali. He has been in France for nearly twenty years, and he promises her that he will return soon. The French are sometimes racist toward him, he says, but he doesn't let it get to him. She asks him about his sniffling. "I'm fixing a car outside and it's cold," he explains.

In the film's most affecting sequence, the camera is trained on a woman in a yellow headscarf riding the train. Diop speaks in voiceover about the home movies her sister shot of their family—a total of eighteen minutes. These are among the few images she has of her mother, a cleaner who each morning left home before Diop had woken up. "I search for traces of my mother," she muses. "She's always a silhouette on the edge of the frame, ready to disappear." Diop is speaking about the Hi-8 footage which we now see—the family preparing, then settling down to enjoy a Christmas dinner—but also the elusive figure her mother cuts in this work, and, perhaps, an indication of the enigmatic mothers that will show up in her later film *Saint Omer* (2022). The image washes over in interlaced static, when another picture emerges. Her sister had recorded these "events of which no trace remains" over a copy of *The Wild One* (1953): Marlon Brando scowls from his motorcycle, and rides off.

With these words, *Nous* starts to appear differently, its absences as palpable as its presences. What is there seems so often to point to what is gone: snippets of movies, parents missed in the morning or on film, lonely pensioners, and in a particularly haunting segment, a gallery exhibition of the Jews of that quarter who were sent to concentration camps. The "non-place" Diop describes of the communities around the RER B is also something within her characters, that which passed unnoticed, or wasn't valued. For Diop, it is her own family history, the mundane moments of which so little remains. Diop speaks with author Pierre Bergounioux, who shares her interest in those who go unseen, or what he calls "folk who had lived, existed, without ever finding any traces or reflections of themselves or their lives in the pages of books, or in images that appear on screens." *Nous* is not an attempt to restore what has been lost, but a way of indicating, in time and along the train route, something of the many people who have passed through this place, and for a moment, made it theirs.

Itinerary

Los Angeles to Rhinecliff

In *No Data Plan* (2019), Miko Revereza travels from Los Angeles to Rhinecliff, New York, by train. Though it is cheaper and faster to go by plane, Amtrak does not require passengers to show their government-issued IDs. For Revereza, an undocumented immigrant who moved from the Philippines to California at the age of five, this relative anonymity is a necessity.

Revereza's special status under the Deferred Action for Childhood Arrivals (DACA) Act, signed into law during the Obama administration, expired shortly after Trump took office in his first term. No longer eligible for federal financial aid, he wrote directly to university administrators to see if they would make good on their promise to enroll and protect undocumented students. Among the offers he received, Revereza accepted the one from Bard College, in Upstate New York. *No Data Plan* tracks an otherwise ordinary journey of a college student returning to campus. But because of Revereza's undocumented status, the train ride completely transforms. Every station stop risks exposure and subsequent deportation, and the tedium of the nearly three-day journey becomes a prolonged state of paranoia.

No Data Plan inverts the tropes of long-distance train movies, especially those set in the American West. There are countless examples of rail-bound adventure: Cary Grant could be framed as, then assume the identity of, a spy aboard the 20th Century Limited in *North By Northwest* (1959) (as he explains to Eva Marie Saint, the train is safer than a plane because it offers more places to hide); Jack Lemmon and Tony Curtis could simultaneously flee mobsters and pursue a ukelele-wielding Marilyn Monroe aboard a Miami-bound Pullman car in *Some Like It Hot* (1959); Johnny Depp could startle at the sound of shotguns fired from the carriage window at grazing buffalo in *Dead Man* (1995); and Joel McCrea, playing an out-of-touch screenwriter who hits the road to experience the real America, could wind up in a cattle car in *Sullivan's Travels* (1941). You could expect just about anything aboard a westward train, except boredom.

Amtrak, the country's semi-public railway (less commonly, it is called the National Railroad Passenger Corporation), opened in 1971, and today serves roughly twenty-three million passengers annually. Its furnishings may be more humble, its timetables less dependable, its amenities lacking, but still it retains something of the allure of its nineteenth- and early twentieth-century predecessors. Some of this trades on fiction, that the American railroad is an expression of the nation's democratic ideals. This view is sometimes perpetuated from outside the country. As Belgian detective Hercule Poirot observes of his fellow passengers—and murder suspects—in Agatha Christie's *Murder on the Orient Express* (adapted for film by Sidney Lumet in 1974, and again by Kenneth Branagh in 2017): "I tried to imagine whether such an assembly were ever likely to be collected under any other conditions. And the answer I made to myself was—only in America. In America there might be a household composed of just such varied nationalities—an Italian chauffeur, and English governess, a Swedish nurse, a French lady's maid and so on."

The reality is that the American train was a highly segregated and stratified space in the nineteenth and early twentieth centuries. For a newly arrived immigrant, the places where one could ride a train might change along a single journey. If a person arrived at Ellis Island from Italy, Poland, or Russia, for example, they would wait in a separate area to board, apart from American citizens, then travel in a retrofitted boxcar until Chicago. At that point in the journey, because railroad companies viewed newly arrived immigrants as potential settlers, their situation improved. Class allowed relative mobility, at least for white passengers: If a European immigrant could afford a first-class fare, they would be allowed to mix with others in that compartment. Such accommodations were unavailable to non-white passengers, however. Chinese immigrants, no matter their wealth, were prohibited from such spaces, as were Black passengers in the South.[1] The only time Black people were not confined to segregated compartments was as workers, chiefly porters. When he was not yet seventeen, Malcolm X worked as a dishwasher and porter aboard trains in the Northeast. On and off the train, he encountered considerable discrimination, but he was also able to discover a vibrant Black community in Harlem. These experiences were formative for his later thinking about racial inequality in the United States.[2]

If there could be said to be such a thing as "Amtrak charm," it animates Albert Maysles's last documentary *In Transit* (2015), where chatty strangers share intersecting journeys on the Empire Builder, an especially scenic line that runs between Chicago and Seattle. Onboard, an impromptu, even bucolic community forms: A perpetually shoeless kid asks a man about his tattoos, a young Black father shares stories with an elder who had met Martin Luther King Jr., a photographer befriends an expectant mother who is three days overdue. This last passenger, on her way to family after trouble with her partner, understandably unsettles the staff—though, as one more seasoned crew member recalls, something similar once happened before, and the baby was delivered by an Amish midwife. Everyone seems to be looking further than they normally do, to unknown futures, to pasts they are ready to release. Maybe it's the landscape, which stretches for miles under an enormous sky. Or maybe it's the train itself, which, between two points of consequence, feels weightless by comparison. "I've always been a wife, a mother, somebody's daughter, somebody's something. . . . I was just me on the train," one woman breathes. Another, returning from a joyful reunion with a daughter she'd been forced to give up for adoption, sports a head of newly dyed hair—bright red—a tattoo, and a huge smile.

The train inspires freedom, except for those it doesn't. Aboard the Empire Builder, the conductor asks a passenger for their ID, then laughs and says he's just kidding. A nearly identical scenario in *No Data Plan* plays out very differently. This time the conductor is far more stern. "It's never been a rule," she says dryly, "[but] if you know me, you know that I always ask for ID." Revereza cuts to his own darkened seat, his ticket pulled up on his phone. The moment passes in a cut; we assume he's ok, if only because the movie continues. But it's easy to imagine how each of these mundane encounters would send him into a mute panic. This is how he films: close to his body, crouched down, narrow. His attention is folded inward, and the camera looks to what is most immediate. He shoots the frayed rip in his jeans, or the seam of a leather seat. Often he films the window, but not the view outside, which is usually blurred. Instead he studies its surface, on which passengers have left impressions of their hands and faces.

Against the norms of adventurous long-distance train films, *No Data Plan* charts an interior journey. Revereza hardly speaks; instead his voice comes across through text that appears at the bottom of the frame, most of it detailing his mother's affair with a young rideshare driver, with whom she eventually decides to run away to Nebraska. Much of the film is quiet, with muffled snatches of conversation and the ever-present rattling of the train. Occasionally we hear voiceovers, evidently recorded at another time. These, too, point to distant pasts and futures. In one, Revereza's aunt regrets the family's lowered class standing since coming to the United States, and surmises that his father would by now be the vice president of a bank had they not emigrated. Revereza himself recounts a dream he had of arriving in Manila and being unable to leave the airport. There is no resolution to any of these stories, only ambiguity and deferral.

Accordingly, there is a dialectical alternation between two types of shots. The first are still and long, carefully composed, even sculptural. But the apparent stasis of these moments is undercut by the second type of shot: the handheld, furtive views that Revereza records when other people are around. Though he is nervous, he also admits, in a phone call, that he has frequently imagined the scenario in which he is finally caught. He greets it with calm. The film lurches between boredom and terror, each leading into the other, creating an oppressive state of anxious suspension. This can be seen in one of the film's most stunning long takes. Shooting from the end of the train, the camera looks out onto the receding tracks. The train enters a tunnel, and daylight is cut to a small aperture in the center of the frame. For over a minute, it dims and shrinks. In the darkness, it seems to float. Revereza fixes on the spot of light, an act that feels like holding one's breath. As the dot fades into the darkest shade of gray shy of black, the other end abruptly overtakes the image, suddenly bright and crisp, and marked with a post that reads "New Mexico." This moment of relief gives way to the realization that there is still so far to go.

At the Buffalo/Depew stop, near the end of the journey, the tone shifts. An otherwise benign view of a parking lot is interrupted by a cut, then the sudden ducking of the camera below the window. A moment of darkness. Then a close-up of Revereza's leg, his hand visibly clenched. As he cowers, we hear his voice, apparently speaking on the phone. "Um, did you see my Story?" he asks softly. He narrates what has happened: The two cars closest to the train were border patrol vehicles, and Revereza spotted agents walking to the train. The moment he has been dreading seemed to have arrived. "Fuck, this is it, this is where they catch up to me."

He then pulls out his phone and films the Instagram Story he shared. For the entire trip, he has avoided using Wi-Fi and cellular data, in part to avoid detection, but at this moment

everything shifts. In the Story, over images of the border patrol cars, he has written "I'm ok [crying face emoji]" and "wtf is America." Another slide advances. His face appears, for the first time in the film, a refracted image, slightly blurred in the screen of the phone. He clicks through his Stories, his thumb pausing to hold onto the image of his face. His words are blunt and direct, both the mute text in the Story, and, moments later, the account given over the phone. The agents walked through his compartment, and, as he describes, they were looking for "anyone that looks like an immigrant." Miraculously, they passed by him. His voice rises. "I decided right then and there, there's no doubt in my mind. I'm out. I'm just fucking over it. I've been here my whole life and I'm still a fugitive here. I don't need this shit anymore."

Revereza has described himself as a "stateless artist," simultaneously an artist without a state, and one persecuted by the state. Such artists carry a unique burden: "stateless artists must contort themselves into meticulous performances of evasion."[3] For necessary reasons, their work is clandestine, oblique, blurry, and poorly exposed. They "must be strategic about how their visibility is negotiated," especially when the work is so personal, and so potentially revealing, as with *No Data Plan*. How does one film without compromising safety? Or, as Revereza asks, "How does an undocumented documentary filmmaker document themself?"[4]

The answer, at least in part, is to shift the terms of what is documented. He writes: "A film is an act of seeing that makes itself seen, an act of hearing that makes itself heard, an act of physical and reflective movement that makes itself reflexively felt and understood."[5] In other words: Step back from the scenario to see the person filming it. Peel back the layers of obfuscation to understand why they needed to be there. See the stateless artist in a way that all other modes of seeing disallow. See differently. See something else.

To create his film *Biometrics* (2019), made the same year as *No Data Plan*, Revereza repeatedly pressed his inked finger onto a long strip of clear 16mm leader. The result is a direct animation of his fingerprints, inspired by the many times he had to register his fingerprints to maintain his DACA status. The image is abstract, but also highly sensitive. Revereza maintains strict conditions for the film's screening: It can only be shown with him present, and it can never be digitized, because failing either requirement would significantly raise the risk of his capture. This is a film that, for political reasons, can rarely be seen. Its viewership is necessarily small, and so far, I have not yet had opportunity to see it. So I imagine it, a rush of color and smudges, like a rollicking river. The imagination may be the only possible place for a stateless cinema to truly flourish. A refuge, perhaps, but there is a utopian impulse in this too. A place of freedom and permission. A place where there is no need to hide. A world without borders.

3

Phantom Rides

Consider the name of that early cinema genre, the phantom ride. In such films, a camera was affixed to the front of a moving vehicle, most often a train or a roller-coaster car. Such a view would glide through the landscape, the track ahead clear of any obstruction. It gave the viewer a virtual experience of being on the train. But it also raised a discomfiting question: Who is driving the train? Whose view does this belong to?

Train films frequently play with the sensation of a passenger's loss of control. There are countless examples in which the train overwhelms the protagonist because they are threatened by nefarious actors, because the train is headed to its own climactic disaster, or because escape, especially from a fast-moving train, is all but impossible. Such films heighten a sense of disorientation and delirium. They frequently result in train wrecks. But they typically maintain the protagonist's perspective.

Phantom rides, meanwhile, do not definitively adopt a passenger's point of view. The viewer may be sitting in the driver's seat, but they are not the ones driving the train. Rather an uncanny sensation arises: The *train* is driving the viewer.

Such trains seem to drive themselves. Though they leave the driver's seat empty, the viewer does not really occupy it, as would be the case, say, in a video game. In cinema, one can only phantasmatically sit in its cab. As a type of film, phantom rides provoke the sensation of loss of control, but more unsettling is the way they overtake the viewer's perspective. In its place, they suggest another possibility: train POV.

A phantom ride implies a phantom driver, of course, and there are plenty of train movies that are steered by otherworldly forces. Many of these are horror narratives, from Maxim Gorky's vision of a "kingdom of shadows," discussed in this book's introduction, and various adaptations of Charles Dickens's 1866 short story "The Signal-Man," about a signal worker visited by a ghost prior to several horrific accidents. Train enthusiasts on the r/trains subreddit have joked that the installments of *The Human Centipede* franchise count as train films, but there are more direct examples as well: stranded passengers visited by ghosts in Walter Forde's *The Ghost Train* (1941); the water-skimming commute between a mystical bathhouse and rural Japan in Hayao Miyazaki's *Spirited Away* (2001); and Kim Dong-bin's k-horror film *Red Eye* (2008), in which a demonic spirit joins a modern-day train with cars that previously crashed along the same route. I like to imagine *Red Eye* as a train's revenge for the early cinema fad of deliberately crashing outmoded trains, like the colliding locomotives in Thomas Edison's *Railroad Smashup* (1904), or, payback for the carnage of train disaster films described in Chapter 2. Crumpled trains will come back to haunt you.

Train POV, meanwhile, is more ambiguous and expansive. Watching movies from this perspective—a deliberately speculative exercise, to be sure—means considering trains as characters in, and even directors of, their films. How do trains intervene in people's lives? Orchestrate events? What do they know, and what powers do they hold?

Take the end of Whit Stillman's *The Last Days of Disco* (1998). An otherwise straightforward drama about hard-partying college grads in Manhattan subtly takes leave of realism when Alice (Chloë Sevigny) and Josh (Matt Keeslar) board the New York City subway. The O'Jays's "Love Train" begins to play nondiegetically; it is the end of the film, and this is the time when end credit music would normally come on. Surprisingly, however, the couple seems to hear it, because they begin to dance. After a cut, an even more surprising turn of events: The entire car erupts into dancing (though one man, a true New Yorker, resolutely stays seated with his newspaper). The end credits begin to roll, and behind them the train arrives at Church Avenue to a platform full of dancing people. The O'Jays implore the "people of the world" to "join hands [to] start a love train." On this joyful, fantastical ride, you "don't need no ticket."

The intrusiveness of the train isn't immediately apparent in David Lean's *Brief Encounter* (1945). It is a love story, after all, and not a meticulous choreography by way of train. Most of the film occurs in flashback, as Laura (Celia Johnson) recounts in voiceover the story of her affair with Alec (Trevor Howard), whom she first met at the Milford train station a month prior. She imagines telling the story to her husband Fred (Cyril Raymond), her closest confidante, though of course he can never know the truth. As she revisits the scenes of her romance, she reflects on details she had missed in the moment. About Alec's hand slipping into her arm: "I didn't notice it then but I remember it now." The same could be said of the train's outsized role in the film.

The presence of trains is already a departure from the original one-act stage play by Noël Coward. *Still Life* set the chance meeting and resulting affair between Laura and Alec entirely within the refreshment room at the station. Lean moved much of the action outdoors, most significantly to the platform where the express trains blow by, always at night, accompanied by giant plumes of smoke and a piercing whistle. The rush of the "Flying Scotsman" is what sends Laura indoors to remove a piece of coal grit that landed in her eye. Alec, a doctor, helps remove it. "That's how it all began," she muses. "I completely forgot about it. It didn't mean anything to me at all. At least I didn't think it did." Another memory revised into significance.

The two soon discover that their schedules overlap every Thursday. Laura, a housewife, comes in from Ketchworth to visit the library, shop, and take in a movie. From the opposite direction, Alec, an ambitious doctor from Churley, comes to cover a shift at the Milford hospital. The local trains bring them together, but the film lingers on their separations. As with the eye-grit incident, their meetings are always marked by departures. Alec's train leaves first, at 5:40 p.m., three minutes ahead of Laura's on the opposite platform. The timetable is fixed, the trains never late, and the lovers are the ones who must adjust to their schedules. "You'll miss your train," Laura quietly urges Alec after he asks to see her again.

Missing the train has grave consequences. On what would be their last encounter, Laura boards her usual train, then at the last moment, she bounds off. Alec has stayed on at a colleague's empty flat, and she rushes there, presumably to

consummate their affair. But the colleague unexpectedly returns, causing Laura to flee down the back stairs. After wandering in the rain for several hours, she returns to the station to catch the last train home. The train's regularity in this instance offers a chance for Alec to catch up with her. But even their last cup of tea is thwarted when a nosy friend spots Laura and plops herself down at their table. This is a scene that plays twice in the film—in the beginning, without any context for the sad looks the lovers exchange, and now, at its devastating conclusion, the mute awareness that both of them share, that this is the end of their affair. The arrival of the Churley train is announced over a loudspeaker. "I must go," Alec says. "Yes, you must," Laura replies. As he leaves, he gently squeezes her shoulder.

While the friend prattles on, Laura rushes out to the platform, her hair whipped by the passing express train. Harsh light flashes across her stricken face. In voiceover, she admits she nearly threw herself onto the tracks, but wasn't brave enough to follow through. Instead she returns to the refreshment room, to the friend who insists that she and Laura ride back to Ketchworth together, and finally to Fred, who glances up from his crossword puzzle to see his wife's still troubled face. "You've been a long way away. Thank you for coming back to me," he says with a disarming knowingness, as though, all along, he had been listening to Laura's voiceover confession. As if each of her trips to Milford had added up to a single railway journey that now was looping back to him.

Sometimes the train seems to know more than the characters do. In Hong Sangsoo's *The Power of Kangwon Province* (1998), Jisook (Oh Yun-hong) travels by train to the mountains of Kangwon Province, accompanied by two girlfriends. She is unaware that Sangkwon (Baek Jong-hak), who until recently was her boyfriend, is aboard the same train. Like *Brief Encounter*, the film features a scene twice viewed: The first is of Jisook standing in the aisle of a crowded car, visibly annoyed as a porter passes through with a snack cart. A middle-aged man in glasses elbows past her to buy beer and dried squid. Midway through the film, the moment recurs, this time from the opposite perspective. Only the back of Jisook's head is visible. Now the pushy man is in the foreground, and after he grabs his food, the camera follows his return to his much roomier cabin, where he joins Sangkwon. "This train is packed with girls!" he grins. Jisook and Sangkwon continue their separate journeys, each unaware of the other. Like a pair of weak magnets, they are drawn to but also just miss each other, at the same sashimi restaurant, or encountering the same woman who is later found dead at the bottom of a cliff. Strangest of all is a pair of goldfish that Sangkwon's neighbor had given to him prior to his Kangwon sojourn. When he returns, one of them is gone. Could it be the same misplaced fish that Jisook finds on a trail, so far from the water? Their staggered arrivals—right place, but always the wrong time—is similar to the way they ride the inbound train. They are together in a sense, but shunted off in separate cars.

With *Café Lumière* (2003), Hou Hsiao-Hsien's ode to Yasujirō Ozu on the centenary of the Japanese director's birth, both the film and characters are drawn to the labyrinthine train systems of Tokyo, and especially Ochanomizu Station, where four separate rail lines overlap. For a train enthusiast like Hajime (Tadanobu Asano), it is the most marvelous place in the city, and it is where he asks Yoko (Yo Hitoto) to meet him. But on her way there, she starts to feel sick, and gets out at Shinjuku. They do not make it to Ochanomizu.

Later, she explains offhandedly that she's pregnant. She doesn't say more, and Hajime doesn't press. He is more comfortable listening, as he does when he records the sounds of trains across the city. By comparison, Yoko, a writer searching for traces of the expat Taiwanese composer Jiang Wenye, is direct and talkative. This causes considerable grief for her stepmother, who frowns when Yoko explains that she won't marry the child's father, a Taiwanese man, because he is too close to his mother. Meanwhile her father expresses his worry through slow sips of sake and heavy sighs.

The connection between Yoko and Hajime is ambiguously romantic. Hajime helps her locate sites once frequented by

Jiang, and he gives her a copy of Maurice Sendak's *Outside Over There*, a children's book that closely resembles a dream Yoko recently had. At home she reads it: A girl, distracted, does not notice when her baby sister is stolen by goblins, and replaced with a replica made of ice. Yoko also offers gifts: a delivery of coffee from a nearby restaurant, and a pocket watch which she sets by peering at the dashboard of a train driver's cab. That same watch reappears in an illustration Hajime shows to Yoko on his laptop. It is strung around the neck of an infant surrounded by trains. "It's a womb of trains!" Yoko exclaims. Then, pointing at the baby in the center: "Is that you?" He nods. "The eye seems kind of lonely," she says. "Yes, close to tears," he murmurs.

My mention of these three infants—Yoko's unborn child, the kidnapped sibling of her dream, and the baby Hajime in the womb of trains—might make them seem more pronounced than they are in the film. But the experience is more like seeing telephone poles outside the window of a moving train, noticeable if not especially remarkable. Though Yoko is the film's central figure, the deep-focus cinematography constantly reminds us of all that is happening around her as she moves through the city on foot or riding its trains. In especially crowded spaces, it is easy to lose sight of her, a slight figure in a pageboy cap. The potential romance between Yoko and Hajime might just as easily be missed, not only by the viewer, but by the two characters themselves. Only from the perspective of the train can we begin to glimpse it.

In one particularly astounding shot, Yoko stands at the door of a train, looking out through the window. When it pulls into a station, another train arrives on the opposite side of the platform. As the trains match in speed, it is possible to see into the arriving one. The camera pulls away from Yoko to find, through the blur of the platform crowd, and into the other train, Hajime standing with his microphone raised. Though he is listening intently, he does not see Yoko. Nor does she see him, even though it would take only a half step for her to join with the camera view. Another time, Hajime boards a train and finds, to his surprise, Yoko dozing in her seat. He moves toward her, a tender look on his face. She does not wake up.

Perhaps this is why Hou favored Ochanomizu Station, which appears three times in the film. In each of the shots, multiple trains crisscross each other: the orange cars of the JR Chuo Rapid Line that hug the Kanda River, the yellow-striped Sobu Line trains that run across the Shohei Bridge, and the red Marunouchi Line subway cars that emerge from

a tunnel. These are the kinds of overlaps where Hajime and Yoko, each traveling separate paths, might finally converge.

Sigmund Freud identified the motif of missing one's train as a common form of the anxiety dream. In some cases, the anxiety is about death: "Dreams of missing a train . . . are dreams of consolation for another kind of anxiety felt in sleep—the fear of dying. 'Departing' on a journey is one of the commonest and best authenticated symbols of death."[1] Maybe this is why the difference between a missed and made train is so pivotal in Krzysztof Kieślowski's *Blind Chance* (1987). (Its confused Hollywood cousin *Sliding Doors* (Peter Howitt, 1998), plays on the motif but without significant consequence. It is true that Helen (Gwyneth Paltrow) dies in one of the timelines, but, by the romantic comedy logic of the film, it is far more important that she meet the love of her life, which she manages to do in both. At least the version of her that makes the train gets an interesting haircut.)

Blind Chance starts with a close-up of a man's scream at the moment of his death. This is the howl that Witek (Bogusław Linda) makes before his airplane explodes midair. We only know this in retrospect, after Witek has passed through three different scenarios of a fateful train bound for Warsaw many years prior. Each of his life trajectories—becoming a Communist Party stooge, joining an underground ring of political dissidents, and returning to medical school to enjoy life as a bourgeois doctor—depends on a few key moments inside the Łódź station: he makes the train, he doesn't but knocks into a station agent, he doesn't and avoids the station agent. We know little about Witek prior to this seemingly random string of events. His domineering father has recently passed away, leaving him, over the phone, the enigmatic message: "you don't have to." The open-endedness of those final words is anything but liberating. To paraphrase Sartre, Witek lives a life condemned to be free, with each path radically different from the others, and with no apparent core other than a confused and searching young man. He is like a different person in each life: In one he is betrayed, while in another he is the betrayer. He has a family, or lives alone. He is baptized, or remains an avowed atheist. He lives comfortably, or is penniless.

All three storylines end up at the airport, before the departure of a plane to Paris. Only the last Witek—the smug doctor—actually makes it on board. Astute viewers might recognize the leather headrest from the film's opening shot. The film cuts to a wide exterior view of the plane as it takes off, grows smaller, then erupts into flames. The scream that begins the film can now be understood as Witek's horror, replaying, in an instant, not just the events of his life, but *all* his lives.

At the end of the film, we can now understand its beginning. Following Witek's scream, the camera plunges into the cavity of his mouth. This recalls a similar ingestion from James Williamson's *The Big Swallow* (1901), in which a man sitting for a photographic portrait approaches the camera and eats it. It is a cinematic ouroboros: The gaping hole at the end of Witek's life leads to the moment of his birth. The shot that follows the plunge into his mouth is a traumatic scene from a hospital ward in the midst of a violent uprising, which left Witek's mother and twin brother dead. Describing this scene to one of his lovers, he says, "I feel like I remember that moment. It's like an image beneath my eyelids."

The hospital scene and the other shots that follow Witek's scream are not just flashbacks, but memories that float up between spaces of black, and with the rarely used device of first-person camerawork in which characters look directly at the camera, which we understand to be Witek's perspective. Witek himself is mostly unseen. The camera pans and tilts with his movements as if it were his own eyes. There he is as a boy, looking at his reflection in the mirror. When Witek's father sternly instructs him in his studies, the camera dutifully lowers to the paper on the table before it, where the boy's hand writes out a number. A later memory shows his arm reaching from behind the camera to grasp a woman's hand as she steps down from an embankment.

This first-person camerawork shifts once the film enters the first of its three timelines. From then on, it adopts a more conventional third-person perspective, with Witek usually visible in frame. Ordinarily, such a POV would be unremarkable. But because of this earlier sequence, and the occasional intrusion of one of its memories into the stream of events, it feels especially impersonal, like it is not Witek's. Whose perspective, then, is it? Could it belong to the train, which, after all, is the only constant in his life? In each timeline, Witek seeks belonging and purpose. But the train exposes the randomness of his choices, cynically suggesting that there is no meaningful difference between a party bureaucrat and a Catholic dissident in Soviet-controlled Poland. While the train is all-seeing, Witek can only intuit this at a few key moments. In the second scenario, he says to his mentor Stefan, a priest: "If I hadn't missed a train a month ago, I wouldn't be here now." Stefan assures him it's not chance. Witek persists: "Sometimes I think it is."

Against the cold indifference of Kieślowski's train, the one in *No Man of Her Own* (Mitchell Leisen, 1950) seems to take pity on penniless and pregnant Helen (Barbara Stanwyck). We meet her desperate to reunite with her loutish boyfriend Steve, who has holed up in a New York apartment with a tawdry blonde. As Helen weeps from outside the door, he slips her a one-way ticket back to San Francisco. She has no choice but to board the train. It is crowded and hot, and Helen flops down on her suitcase. But then a stroke of luck, or train providence—a man offers her his seat next to his wife Patrice (Phyllis Thaxter), who is also expecting. The newlywed couple takes kindly to Helen, and before long they are chatting merrily together in the dining car. Later, in the powder room, Patrice asks Helen to hold a ring with her and Hugh's names on it, because she is afraid of losing it. She encourages Helen to put it on her finger, and Helen warily obliges.

Just then, the train's whistle blows, and the car begins to shake violently. The mirror reflection of Helen wearing Patrice's ring cracks and crashes to the ground. The train is in the throes of derailment, and it tosses the two women together like socks in a dryer. Patrice, Hugh, and their unborn baby all die in the crash; Helen and her child survive. When Helen awakens in a hospital, she is stunned to learn that her baby has been born, and that she has been misidentified as Patrice. For the sake of her infant, she decides to keep her new identity and move in with her wealthy in-laws, who have yet to meet their son's bride.

Moments before the crash, there's an additional superimposition of Helen's profile in close-up in the mirror. It makes no perspectival sense; Patrice is standing too far away for this to be her view, and there is no one else in the room. Could it be the train's? The two overlapped images of Helen in the mirror signal the doubling that will later occur between the two women, as well as the splitting that inevitably follows, like when Helen accidentally writes her own name instead of "Patrice" while shopping for a new pen, a gaffe that her brother-in-law William (John Lund) notices.

In moments like this, *No Man of Her Own* flirts with the conventions of the imposter plot. But something stranger is going on, as the film, and the train in particular, seem intent on bestowing the gift of a new life to Helen. William not only relinquishes his suspicions, but falls in love with Helen, just like the rest of his family. When Steve eventually shows up with a blackmail scheme, William goes to extraordinary lengths to protect Helen, even becoming an accomplice when Helen shoots and kills her ex-boyfriend (or so she believes). After he throws Steve's corpse rather poetically on top of a passing train, he passionately declares to her, "I don't care who you are or what you've done. As far as I'm concerned you were born the night I met you."

While it is admittedly fanciful to imagine the train orchestrating the events that lead Helen to Patrice's family, it is hard to ignore its outsized presence in the film. The train seems to magically appear at key moments in Helen's life. Sometimes this occurs in the form of a whistle, such as the one that is heard after Helen receives a menacing telegram from Steve. As an instrument of fate, the train is rather blunt. It mostly traffics in destruction. But who can deny that it has successfully delivered Helen to her new and happy, if not entirely rightful, home?

* * *

If other films are dominated by train POV, James Benning's *RR* (2007) is steered by a chorus of them. The film's title describes its topic—the railroad—along with its orientation. Road signs marked "RR," usually with a cross between them, signal to a motorist that a train crossing is up ahead. If a train is passing through, it always asserts the right of way. Trains similarly assert their right of way in Benning's film, effectively directing the film more than Benning himself, because each of the forty-two shots is determined, roughly, by the amount of time it takes for a train to cross the frame. This lasts as long as seven and a half minutes, with a train of grain-hopper cars that first enters then crosses over a tunnel in Tehachapi, California, and as short as a matter of seconds, when a work truck speeds down the tracks across a Hudson River bridge in Bear Mountain, New York.

RR is unlike other of Benning's films from the same period, where the film apparatus transparently determines shot subject and length. Both *TEN SKIES* (2004) and *13 LAKES* (2004) feature ten-minute shots, numbering ten and thirteen respectively, with the latter evenly dividing the frame between lake and sky. *casting a glance* (2007), which Benning filmed concurrently with *RR*, adheres to a rule of one-minute shots, and it narrows its attention to a single site. But in *RR* the durational conceit is completely trampled by the train, which offers an alternative structure to Benning's mathematically schematized world.

What appears as a rule is almost immediately broken: Shots start and end with trains, except when the camera lingers ahead of or after the train. Trains pass through, except the few times when they stop. All of the trains are freighters, except the commuter and Amtrak trains that appear. There are no visible people, except a brakeman that steps into frame, and a driver whose forearm hangs out of a sedan window at a suburban railroad crossing. This latter shot occurs early in the film, when a viewer is still figuring out its logic, all while waiting for this train. Its length is finite, but unknown. Impatience breeds. *How much longer is this going to take?*, a viewer might wonder, just like the driver stuck at the railroad crossing. Or Benning himself, who said about the Kansas City Southern train, which only crosses the spillway at Lake Pontchartrain in LaPlace, Louisiana once weekly, "I'm at the mercy of the train. It's kind of like fishing."[2] The train decides when the shot is over.

Allan Sekula observes that in RR, "durational authority is ceded to a more powerful machine, and in doing so suggests that not everything in the world of things and actions is given over to the tyranny of the signifier."[3] Instead the signified, the train, barrels through, with Benning trailing behind. The train also makes new demands on the camera. In most films, shot lengths are organized according to a human figure—a wide shot will show a person from head to toe, a medium shot will depict them from the mid-thigh up, and a close-up will frame the shoulders and head. RR demands a different vocabulary, one that centers *trains*. Here a wide shot might mean a significant length of train is visible within the frame, say ten cars, or what amounts to a thin line. A medium shot might show a few cars; a thicker line. And a train close-up would cut off some portion of the top or bottom of the train as it passes.

Sekula notes a subtler but no less riotous way in which RR upends cinematic norms, which is to upset its spatial geometry.

While RR's framings adhere to classical landscape convention, which locates a level horizon line in the center of the frame, the trains refuse to comply. Instead they cut through along the z-axis, sometimes subtly, just by a few degrees, and other times dramatically, charging up or down the frame. This recalls *L'Arrivée d'un train en gare de La Ciotat*, a favorite among experimental filmmakers including, in addition to Benning, Peter Tscherkassky and Thom Andersen. In the Lumières's film, the locomotive moves into frame, and not merely across it. It threatens to exceed the boundaries of the screen. The train-directors of *RR* seem to be aware of this dynamic. The second shot, from Bagdad, California, features a train that (in a train-wide) ventures right across the frame, then cuts toward the camera. When a train does adhere to the horizon line, like the dotted line of black cars moving across a gray stretch of prairie in Champlin, Utah, the graphic pattern renders the shot abstract, like a painting by Mark Rothko. Sekula calls these repeated z-axis intrusions the "compulsive serial repetition of the shattering of the pastoral scene."[4] This has a pointed political purpose: What appears as nature has actually been carved up and reorganized through industry. Or, what art claims as its domain has long been settled by the train.

This interpretation adds heft to RR's playful violations of aesthetic norms. Benning puts the film's trains in historical relief through the addition of select sound clips: President Eisenhower's farewell address warning of future conflict; Gregory Peck reading from the Book of Revelations; the sound of a Huey helicopter, commonly used during the Vietnam War; and NWA attesting to ongoing police violence. America sounds different and darker in these moments. Even the Mormon Tabernacle Choir's rendition of "Battle Hymn of the Republic," heard in the first shot, inclines more toward war than to salvation. The trains of RR, meanwhile, look like they come out of these receding histories. The cars are rusted and tagged with graffiti. Nothing looks new.

But in this film, the sounds of the train are almost always present, as if it never stopped running during all that time. One of the places where Benning films is a nondescript stretch of farmland in Elburn, Illinois. Just looking at the shot, one probably wouldn't know that this was the site of Elburn Farm Co-op, one of the nation's oldest farming collectives, founded in 1921. Later in the film, as a double-decker skirts the edge of a rice field in Nelson, California, we hear Woody Guthrie singing a rare verse from "This Land Is Your Land":

There was a big high wall there that tried to stop me.
The sign was painted, said "Private Property."
But on the backside, it didn't say nothing.
This land was made for you and me.

These lyrics never made it into the version printed in 1950s schoolbooks, and it's easy to understand why. How unruly would it have been for children to learn that the walls and signs that demarcate space are only imaginary? Having passed through Elburn, we see that the country could have been organized differently. The train, that violator of gridded space, is maybe the best carrier for this message. But it's also a groaning, chugging mess of sound, drowning out as much as it makes audible. As soon as it passes, it is gone. The train may have vast reach over the land, but it is a poor historian. It retains nothing. The cargo it holds—oil, grain, automobiles, and whatever is concealed by container—will eventually be delivered, and the train will be empty, again.

If there can be such a thing as train perspective, then surely the thing the train sees would look like a movie. In *Geyserland* (2003), for instance, Mary Ellen Strom mounted projectors from within a moving train. For twenty-five miles, these cast images onto the darkened landscape of the Bozeman Pass in Montana: a view from the train, but also one conceivably for the train. Bill Brand's *Masstransiscope* (1980), an installation in the New York City subway, takes this idea further. The work is viewable from the Manhattan-bound B and Q lines just after the Dekalb Station. It is best to sit on the right side of the train. In the tunnel, Brand painted a three hundred-foot panel of brightly colored shapes, illuminated by fluorescent light. Between the train and the painting, he installed a wall with 228 regularly spaced slits, like those of a zoetrope. The passing train activates this apparatus. In fact, it is its crucial element, the motor of this distributed projector. *Masstransiscope* reverses the mechanics of the projection system: Instead of a moving image, it is the viewer who moves, by way of the train. For a few seconds in the subway tunnel, cinema is enacted. Brand's whimsical shapes begin to dance. One looks like a tumbling rhombus. A tangle of noodles wraps around a maroon ball. A squid-like shape blasts off.

Most riders, of course, don't realize that their train has momentarily become a movie. Sometimes people will look up and watch some portion of it, then return to their phones. When people notice the work it is often because a child has made some excited noise about it. This is *Masstransiscope*'s secondary effect, and a clue to its title. It is a view of the mass transit system itself, and especially its riders, who, in New York, are as colorful of characters as the wobbly animations outside their window. Watching *Masstransiscope* means, on some level, watching other people, to see who else saw this burst of color and movement. To catch the eye of a stranger during its passage is like sharing a secret.

Itinerary

Shanghai to Hong Kong

With trains, there is a persistent sense of nostalgia, and of childhood in particular. Is this because we remember the strangeness and delight of the window view from our earliest train trips? And why the appeal of toy train sets, if not for their miniaturized worlds, graspable in a way the adult one is not? In an interview, Chantal Akerman compared the rocking motion of trains to the experience of the womb: "We experience the sensual aspect of trains when we're in the cinema, when we're close to our mother . . . "[1] It is a sensation that lulls and provokes dreaming, qualities the train shares with cinema.

Trains, films, and the dreams of a child come together in Bruce Conner's *Valse Triste* (1979). A boy gets into bed and turns off the light. He closes his eyes. The image fades to black and, after a pause, returns on a shot of a steam locomotive as it lurches forward. The train begins his dream, or is it the other way around? What follows is a montage of found footage, with space of black between shots, as though to suggest the disconnected nature of dream imagery. Among its shots, *Valse Triste* shares one of a crumbling hunk of granite with another of Conner's films, *Take the 5:10 to Dreamland* (1976), a title that makes explicit the connection to trains. This shot and others convey a sense of gradual overwhelm, from a large bonfire that a boy helps to build, a rapidly spinning windmill, a hose spilling water over a gravel road, and, in the film's haunting final shot, a procession of cars driving slowly through floodwaters. The sleeping boy never reappears. We leave the film still in murky depths of the dream, the train still presumably rolling.

A train is what crosses the border between dreams and waking in Harun Farocki's *Bedtime Stories: Railways* (1977), one of many short films he made for children for German television.[2] In each of the films, his twin daughters Anna and Lara, lying in their shared bed, ask each other, "what are you imagining now?" They trade descriptions of seemingly fantastical sights: a ship crossing the street, a train gliding over a river. After each turn, Farocki cuts to footage of the mechanical marvels that match their words. In *Railways*, one girl is too tired to continue, and she dramatically plops her pillow over her head. A moment later she is dreaming that she is on a train. She continues the description of what she sees: "I step onto my locomotive and drive away." In the cab, she turns the speed control wheel, and her sister joins her. They ride together, their eyes wide as they look out the window. Farocki cuts back to their bedroom, where both girls are asleep.

Tiffany Sia's *A Child Already Knows* (2024) similarly mixes train travel and a child's patchy memory. Onscreen we see a series of cartoon animals, a stop-motion pond, and miniature homes and forests that offer a world of fantasy and play. There is just enough danger to keep things interesting. A wolf stalks a baby bunny, two birds lift a frog high into the air. Occasionally the stream of images is interrupted by title cards, white lettering on black backgrounds, which explain, among other things, that we are seeing animations from Shanghai Television, the state broadcasting company, that aired between the years 1945, the end of the Second Sino-Japanese War, and 1966, the start of the Chinese Cultural Revolution. Another card notes that these are the years of Sia's father's childhood, when he lived in Shanghai until his family escaped, first to the southern city of Hangzhou, then to Guangzhou, and finally to Hong Kong, where her grandfather had already been living for some time.

There is something about the movement and sound of a train that can lead us back to our younger days, especially on an overnight journey. This sensation was described by Fritz Lang when discussing the inspiration for *Woman in the Moon* (1929):

> I can lie for hours, hands under my head, and stare into the night. The rolling of the wheels which has for me an ever new changing rhythm, the soft movement of the body, the whistle of the locomotive, the swarms of falling stars of its sparks, the consciousness to be carried from one place to another without having anything else to do but lie still dreaming the dreams of youth . . . all of this combines for me to [sic] a condition of intoxication which inspires me again and again.[3]

Sia's work evokes the train effect Lang describes. The sound of the train is persistent, running through the entirety of the film's thirty-three minutes. At first it is intrusive, then, as any train rider will recognize, it starts to dissipate as white noise. At various moments it seems louder, then quieter, though nothing, in fact, has changed on this journey. The train's rhythmic lull has been constant, even if the attention of the rider—or viewer—has not.

This fading in and out also occurs in the images onscreen. Highly seductive cartoons pull you in, stark white text push you out. "The real film is neither here nor there," a title warns, "but in its interstices." Sia asks us to watch askance, but also into images that "have to be pried open." *A Child Already Knows* demands a form of double vision. Each image is attached to another, from a different moment, as in a chain of loosely associated views. To see them all together is like swimming against a powerful current. It takes considerable wakefulness. It requires a feat of imaginative synthesis.

These are not images Sia's father viewed. He didn't watch television until he was an adult, living in Hong Kong. But Sia adds her own childhood experience to his story, a generational confusion mediated by the captivating power of television images. She writes in her book *On and Offscreen Imaginaries*, "I remember developing an intense attachment to my parents' CRT television in the 1990s; I spent many hours in front of it, unsupervised. So visceral were these experiences, I still vividly remember running my fingers across the monitor and feeling the screen zap with static. . . . My parents were largely absent from my childhood, and the TV took on a constant, avuncular presence."[4] In *A Child Already Knows*, this presence is assumed by the imagined, and heard, train. Its sound is a kind of lullaby: It soothes and masks an otherwise tense situation. The gears churn as the images play like snippets of distant memories. Outside the imaginary window of this film, the landscape is replaced by forest animals that tumble around on state television. A false image, but one you could disappear into. An illusion, or a promise, of safety.

What does the child know? Sia's grandfather was a political refugee, and he left Shanghai for Hong Kong in 1956. Sometime after, her father, just a boy, traveled with his mother on what was disguised as a vacation. The film addresses him in the second person: "you had become aware of the world of adult secrets," reads one card about the family's last days in Shanghai. At the Communist Party banquet hall, he remembers dessert. "The ice cream was the most memorable treat."

Perhaps it is easier to consider what the child does not know. He does not know why he is leaving his home, his piano teacher, the orange cat in the neighbor's yard. He does not know why his father left or why his mother is crying. But he notices things which are relayed by the intertitles: small shipments of butter sent from Hong Kong from his father, a large model ship in the window of the pawn shop where his father sold his winter coat. Such details are consistent with the cartoon images onscreen, at least in scale: a bug that infects the stomach of a man, and a somersaulting boy who rolls off a couch. On the train, inner experience blends with the strange sights outside. For the child who cannot separate the two, or the adult who cannot remember the difference, they all blur together. The child indexes a strange swirl of facts.

Sia writes: "To tell the story of my lineage requires slipping across countries and continents; it goes beyond a naturalized vision of history or a singular national or continental framework. It is the story of port cities fluctuating between cycles of dispossession and affluence, cities where people and materials were bound by brutality even as they were entwined through intimacy."[5] Hong Kong was never meant to be a place where the family would stay, and after Sia turned nine, they moved to the United States. Once in motion, the exile often struggles to find solid ground.

Family history is a broken railway, full of starts and stops. The temptation to connect is apparent in the flow of images, of cartoon creatures narrowly averting danger, and new adventures beginning on the heels of those just concluded. The train rumbles at regular intervals. But Sia holds this binding impulse at a distance. She allows them to break. "These images," a card reads, "serve as proxy for images that are too costly to make, a reenactment in a place of no return." Shanghai is irretrievable. The family can return to no place. Then another card, a dream at least partially dispelled: "but cinema is of the mind anyway."

4

Strangers on Trains

The opening sequence in Alfred Hitchcock's *Strangers on a Train* (1951) begins at ground level, with only people's shoes and the bottoms of their trousers visible. First, a flamboyant pair of shiny wingtip oxfords, called spectator shoes, exits a cab. They're followed by a plain pair of shoes, topped by tweed—though the image is in black and white, I imagine the entire ensemble is brown. The two figures alternate as they enter a train station, then a train, and eventually the same café car, where they accidentally graze each other. Only then does the camera reveal who these characters are: Bruno Antony (Robert Walker), fittingly the one in the spectator shoes, recognizes the other man, Guy Haines (Farley Granger), a professional tennis player and subject of tabloid speculation. Their lives will soon become entangled in an elaborate murder plot proposed by Bruno: they would each kill the person the other man wanted dead, and because of the randomness of their connection, they both would escape the question of motive. "Criss cross," Bruno explains neatly, with a touch of flirtation. Crisscross also describes the parallel editing that

leads to the two characters' chance encounter, when they were just two different pairs of shoes.

The train, like the cinema, is often heralded as a space of social mixing, a microcosm of the city or the nation, where people from dramatically different backgrounds might brush against each other. This democratic ideal has had significant limitations in practice. Previously I discussed the history of train carriages in the United States that were segregated by class, ethnicity, and gender. There is also a prevailing mode of non-interaction, which is to say that passengers are encouraged not to disturb each other, for reasons of safety, propriety, and etiquette. Wolfgang Schivelbusch describes some of the practices that developed in the nineteenth century to navigate this new social space, including an emphasis on reading as a way to avoid direct eye contact with one's oppositely-seated neighbor. Strangers are meant to remain strange. Shoes should just stay shoes.

As Lynne Kirby notes, on a train, "[o]ther people become simply other—transitory presences, mere signifiers without references, bodies bearing no familiar or regular relation to other passengers, bodies likely to disappear at any moment."[1] According to this rule, then, the first transgression committed in *Strangers on a Train* is Bruno's initiation of conversation. Over the course of the film, Guy learns the hard way not to talk to strangers, which is why, at its conclusion, and once again riding a train, his wife stops him from answering another stranger's question: "I beg your pardon, but aren't you Guy Haines?"

Characters in train films tend not to heed this advice. Instead they dive headlong into the escapades that await when passengers chat up their neighbors. Often such encounters are romantic in nature. "You know, every great romance mystery has a train in it," says Beth in *Throw Momma from the Train* (1987), Danny DeVito's off-kilter remake of the Hitchcock film, itself based on a Patricia Highsmith novel. In his version, Guy is Larry (Billy Crystal), an author struggling with writer's block and his ex-wife's success (she goes on *Oprah*!), to the chagrin of Beth, his girlfriend. DeVito plays the Bruno character Owen, a sweet but also amoral simpleton with a mother whose nastiness rivals that of Livia Soprano. Owen lifts the murder plot directly from the Hitchcock film, which happens to be playing at a local theater. "Criss cross," he mumbles incessantly.

But here, Larry and Owen meet in the fiction writing class that Larry is teaching, not on the train. And despite the film's title, no mothers are thrown from trains. Larry, meanwhile, suffers from the onslaught of cartoonish slapstick violence typical of 1980s comedies, including, yes, a tumble off the train. The queer undertones of Bruno and Guy's involvement, underscored by Granger's previous role as the submissive Philip in *Rope* (1948) and the dandyish flourishes of Guy's attire, are here transformed into a goofy romp. Larry finally writes a book about his experience meeting Owen, and Owen pens his own version: a pop-up children's book.

What Beth says is true: Many of the strangers encountered in train films offer the possibility of romance. This goes back at least as far as W.K.L. Dickson's *What Happened in the Tunnel* (1903), already a parody of a common fantasy, where a man takes advantage of the train's combination of relative anonymity and temporary immobility to seduce a beautiful stranger. In Dickson's case, the man who spies a young woman sees his opportunity in the darkness of an approaching tunnel. After the train emerges back into the light, he finds in his arms not the girl, but her Black maid. It's a cheap racist gag, to be sure, but a harbinger for the spontaneous erotic encounters that would prevail in later "romances of the rail." Hitchcock, for instance, explored the erotic potential of alluring strangers on trains in *The 39 Steps*, *The Lady Vanishes*, *Suspicion*, *Saboteur*, *Spellbound*, and *North by Northwest*. As a queer permutation, *Strangers on a Train* also fits the mold. The same idea can be found in the mysterious compartment-mate trying unsuccessfully to leave an abusive relationship in *Night Train (Pociag)* (Jerzy Kawalerowicz, 1959), Gene Tierney's femme-fatalistic introduction on a long-distance train in *Leave Her To Heaven* (John M. Stahl, 1945), and the icy androids aboard a futuristic train in *2046* (Wong Kar-Wai, 2004).

Then there is *Before Sunrise* (1995), perhaps the most commonly mentioned train film suggested to me whenever I told someone I was writing this book. Jesse (Ethan Hawke), a backpacking American, meets the idealistic Céline (Julie Delpy), on a train to Vienna. The film, the first in Richard Linklater's decades-spanning *Before* trilogy, begins as the last entry *Before Midnight* (2013) concludes, with a bickering couple. Céline is trying to read (Georges Bataille's *Story of the Eye*), but is distracted by a loud German couple. So is everyone else in the compartment. She gets up to find a new seat. Her quiet doesn't last long before Jesse, sitting across the aisle, asks her a question. This begins a conversation that will last the entire film, as well as the next two. Though they spend only sixteen minutes of screentime on the train, it sets in motion what will concern the rest of their lives.

None of this would have happened without the train. To start, it places them in a proximity that would have been highly unlikely, with Céline returning from a visit to her grandmother in Bucharest, and Jesse drifting on a Eurail pass after an ignoble breakup in Madrid. More importantly, it also jostles them out of their routines. On the train, Jesse tells Céline, "you have ideas that you ordinarily wouldn't have." His phrasing suggests that the train is not only the happenstance occasion for their meeting, but the catalyst for their ensuing romance. When they arrive at Vienna, where Jesse is scheduled for a flight the next morning, he asks Céline to leave with him. She agrees. Perhaps this is a new idea for her too.

The train promises a different kind of escape for movie star Arindam Mukherjee (played by real-life screen idol Uttam Kumar) in Satyajit Ray's *The Hero* (1966). (The film's plot is echoed by Noah Baumbach's *Jay Kelly* (2025), which casts George Clooney in the role of the aging actor and relocates the train to Italy.) Arindam is at the peak of his career—leaning over its edge, in fact. The reviews for his newest film are not promising, and the fistfight he started the previous night is already in the morning papers. "I just want to escape problems for one full day," he sighs as he packs for an overnight train from Kolkata to Delhi, where he is to receive a prize he does not care about. More than that: He wants to knock himself out on pills and booze, and sleep the entire way. A plane would be too fast. The train gives him time to detach.

Arindam moves as though already encased in that intoxicated bubble. Shielded by a pair of sunglasses, he wafts through the train. Having booked the trip so late, there are no private compartments left, but he doesn't mind sharing. Most passengers gawk, except the elderly Mr. Chatterjee, who tells Arindam that he takes offense to talkies ("on principle") and to alcohol (he is allergic to the smell). No matter for Arindam, who listens with a diffident smile, and walks on.

A woman approaches him in the dining car. Warily, she holds out a piece of paper. It's a request for an autograph. "For a cousin," she quickly asserts. He peers at this bookish woman in thick glasses with curiosity. "You probably haven't seen that many Bengali films," he grins. "Too unrealistic," she replies curtly, then adds before scurrying away, "leading men shouldn't be so godlike."

Arindam seems most compelled by those that are least interested in him. The woman, Miss Sengupta (Sharmila Tagore), returns at the urging of her sister, who wants her to interview Arindam for the women's magazine she edits. He resists, at first, but with benevolence, as a god would do.

"People like me . . . [are] creatures of light and shadow. It's best not to expose those bodies of flesh and blood too clearly to the public eye." It is only later, when he is shaken by a nightmare—him sinking in a pit of cash, surrounded by skeletal hands, his old mentor denying him aid—that he is finally ready to talk.

He finds Miss Sengupta again in the dining car and the interview commences. Arindam, so previously suave and assured, reveals a string of fears and defeats. The train, far from the fantasy of reinvention it provides other passengers, returns him to himself, bare, drunk, and alone. To Miss Sengupta, the stranger to whom he has told everything, he admits, "there's no one I can talk to." The line crystalizes the grief of so many of Ray's male characters, who have made themselves hard and miserable, all while knowing it was entirely their choice. She, on the other hand, descends freely onto the platform when the train arrives in Delhi. In one of the film's few handheld shots, she and her companion, with whom she excitedly chats, pass Arindam. He is surrounded by a crowd of photographers and admirers, once again shielded behind sunglasses and that guarded smile.

In 1995, the doomsday cult Aum Shinrikyo launched a deadly sarin gas attack in the Tokyo subway system, killing thirteen people and injuring thousands. The event profoundly shook the nation. The perpetrators of the attack were executed, its remaining members hunted down, and the group branded an international terrorist organization. This is the backdrop for Hirokazu Kore-eda's *Distance* (2001), his enigmatic follow-up to the international arthouse hit *After Life* (1998). It is unsurprising that a former documentary filmmaker would draw on real-world references, but *Distance* is by no means a typical "inspired by real events" movie.

On the third anniversary of the Ark of Truth disaster, four people gather at a remote lake. They are familiar with each other, but not close. One is a salaryman, another a teacher. There is a florist, and an odd-jobber who spends his earnings at the arcade. What connects them are the people they've lost—each of them was related to a cult member who, after the attack (in the film, the method is a poison released into the water supply), took their own lives. The survivors meet at the train station, then drive together to a nondescript spot at the edge of a forest. There, at the side of the road, they find a parked motorcycle. They hike out to the lake, make small talk, and take turns on the dock to mourn their brother, sister, husband, and wife. Atsushi (Arata Iura), the florist, drops daisies into the water for his sister Yûko. The group enjoys the onigiri packed by Kiyoka, the teacher.

It is hard to pinpoint when things start to get strange. On their way back, they encounter a fifth person, Sakata (Tadanobu Asano), a former cult member who left before the coordinated attack. He accompanies them to the road, only to find the car and his motorcycle missing. They have no reception on their phones, and it is too dark to hike all the way back to the train station. Their only choice is to settle into the cabin where their loved ones once lived together "like family," as Sakata explains. The mood shifts. Their chatter evaporates. Minoru, the salaryman, insists they take off their shoes, despite the "years of dust" that covers everything.

Memories intrude in the quiet. A bare foot stepping across a river stone, a glass of orange juice on a restaurant table, a man bent over the book he is fervently reading. Individually they revisit scenes of departure and disappointment, but the film cuts between these moments as though to create a composite of the pain each of them feels, and also senses in the others. Atsushi asks Sakata about his sister. "She was quiet," Sakata says, and his mind turns to a memory of her at the dock. They are arguing about the end of the world. She is certain it will come soon, while he expresses ambivalence. "I kind of like living here," he says. We also see Atsushi's own memories of Yûko, including one in which they walk together in shallow water, then along a busy road. Looking out over the water, he tells her that "silent blue," when night turns into day, is his favorite time of day. "Is that the end or beginning of the day?" she wonders. Then she adds mysteriously, "I'm in the silent blue, participating in a history that's about to end."

In the morning, the group hikes to town. They make phone calls and slurp noodles. Everyone except Sakata and Atsushi

sleeps on the train. Sakata, standing, leans over Atsushi: "Who are you really?" he asks. Atsushi's mouth opens in surprise. Sakata explains that Yûko told him her brother had committed suicide. Atsushi pauses. "She must have lied," he says tentatively. A voice comes on the loudspeaker: "We are arriving at our final destination." Atsushi is silent. Sakata steps away.

Who is Atsushi? Is he really Yûko's brother? After the companions part ways at the train station, he goes to a hospital where, in the beginning of the film, he had visited an elderly man. Now the bed is empty. A nurse walks in and says the man passed away, and that his real son, not Atsushi, had come in. The mystery deepens. Who is this young man who pretends to be related to people he's not? Why would he, or anyone, wish to join the mourners' private gathering? On the train, the strangers you might encounter could be anyone—a murder accomplice, a future spouse, a mirror of oneself. But in *Distance*, the stranger remains strange to the core, his motives and attachments unknown, and his quiet pauses throwing into doubt all that has come before.

At several points during the film, the characters are shown at the opposite end of an interrogation. (This recalls the interview scenes from *After Life*, which feature many of the same actors.) In the bright light, the faces of the survivors register clearly for the first time; until now they have been seen in profile, in shadow, or in long shot. Atsushi looks surprisingly young in his blue checked shirt. He is asked if he was influenced by the teachings of the cult. His answer is evasive but poetic, which could describe the way we encounter people on trains, strangers with whom we share close quarters, and are then gone: "I don't think I was influenced, but I remember the smell of the lilies vividly."

Midway through Mikio Naruse's *Wife* (1953), the unhappy husband Toichi (Uehara Ken) goes on a business trip with his boss. Both men are relieved to be on the train. "With each minute, we're getting further away from Tokyo and our families," the boss smiles. He takes a sip of whiskey. "it's nice to spread our wings for a change." The ocean shines through the window, wide and inviting.

Toichi's marriage to Mineko (Takamine Mieko) is miserable, as every other scene in this film reminds us. Between them is a suffocating sense of bitterness, but neither is willing to change, either to divorce or to reconcile. Toichi wears his burdens on his shoulders and he slouches in his seat, his tie awkwardly bunched. His more energetic boss keeps the small cups of whiskey flowing. Then he sees something, and motions Toichi to look.

The camera cuts to a wide shot of a young woman (Shiozawa Toyoji, a frequent presence in Naruse's films) in a geometric-print kimono. She is pulling down a suitcase from an overhead bin. "I wonder what type of woman she is," the boss muses. The men guess at her age and occupation. Not a dancer or a housewife; a geisha maybe. If she can hear them, she doesn't make it known. Instead, in the second shot of her, a close-up of her face, she arranges her belongings out of frame. "Looks like she's traveling alone," the boss adds. They continue to watch her and drink.

Brad Stevens observes that this scene would seem to offer the classic setup for the heterosexual male gaze: The men look, the woman is there to be looked at. However, several features complicate this ready paradigm. The woman moves with confidence—she is young, modern, and beautiful. She has means, enough to fill multiple pieces of luggage. She stands, while the men sit. She is without a companion, it is true, but apparently quite comfortable to be traveling alone, and never shares a frame with anyone else, much less the men's cramped two-shot. The beleaguered husbands, meanwhile, can only wonder about her. Stevens notes: "The men, much as they may wish to possess her, are left considering not an unproblematic object of desire, but rather a mystery whose solution stays frustratingly out of reach."[2]

One potential way out of Toichi's dilemma is a flirtation he has begun with Fusako, a young widow who works in his office. She invites him to an exhibition of paintings made by her friend; she too is considering taking up painting. "I envy you," Toichi tells her. But their affair is doomed. Mineko refuses to grant Toichi a divorce, and she eventually confronts and shames Fusako, who then writes a farewell letter to Toichi. Once conjured, the fantasy of the other woman is quickly deflated.

The woman on the train, however, could be considered the *other* other woman. Not a way out for Toichi, but something more like another way altogether. She appears not least like a movie—a creature from an entirely different world. The world she exists in, walled off in her own separate framing, can only be glimpsed and not touched by these men, who will soon return to their unhappy families. But she will

remain, an emissary from an unknowable place. She is a vision conjured by the train, like the blurred seashore outside the window. And when the train arrives at its destination, she will vanish into the crowd.

Acknowledgments

The experience of riding a train, and of watching a film, is often a solitary one. But it can be shared upon reflection. Numerous people recommended train films to me, and I thank all of them: Thom Andersen, Joanna Arnow, Nico Baumbach, Bill Brand, Bill Brown, Edo Choi, Martin Dicicco, Nathan Fitch, Moeko Fujii, Michael Gillespie, Devika Girish, Leo Goldsmith, Sabine Gruffat, Josh Guilford, Alexandre Koberidze, Michael Koresky, Mark Krotov, Sophia Li, Akira Mizuta Lippit, Alice Lovejoy, Michael Metzger, Olaf Möller, Ben Parker, Ray Parker, Dana Polan, Rachael Rakes, Pooja Rangan, Nicolas Rapold, John David Rhodes, Anna Shectman, Daniella Shreir, Tiffany Sia, Stefan Solomon, Dan Sullivan, Anri Vartanov, Pacho Velez, James N. Kienitz Wilkins, Ichiro Yamamoto, Soyoung Yoon, and Damon Young. I am grateful for the readers at Fordham University Press, the invaluable assistance of Mithra Lehn, Sarah Osment, and Patrick Lyons, who accompanied me to La Ciotat. Thomas Lay has supported my work, and this series, from the start. I am especially indebted to Erika Balsom, without whom this space for intelligent, cinephilic, and deeply idiosyncratic writing could not exist. And, more than anyone in the world, I thank Harriet Parker, my most trusted companion no matter the mode of transport. If one is lucky enough to be sitting next to her on the Manhattan-bound B or Q, she might excitedly whisper "the movie!" when the train rattles past Bill Brand's magnificent *Masstransiscope*.

Notes

Introduction: Departures

1 Lynne Kirby, *Parallel Tracks: The Railroad and Silent Cinema* (Duke University Press, 1997), 2.

2 Savoj Žižek in *The Pervert's Guide to Cinema* (Sophie Fiennes, 2006).

3 Lisa Kernan, *Coming Attractions: Reading American Movie Trailers* (University of Texas Press, 2004), 25. Trailers existed in an earlier form dating back to 1912. In 1919, the National Screen Service began a practice of clipping film stills and selling them as advertisements to studios, who then appended them to the ends of films.

4 Taïna Tuhkunen, "Introduction: Railway and Locomotive Language in Film," *Film Journal* 3 (2016): 5, citation on 2.

5 Tuhkunen, "Introduction: Railway and Locomotive Language in Film," 3.

6 See The *Camera Obscura* collective, "*Camera Obscura* at Thirty: Archiving the Past, Imagining the Future," *Camera Obscura* 21, no. 1 (61) (2006): 1–25, citation on 3.

7 See Tom Gunning, "An Aesthetic of Astonishment: Early Film and the (In)Credulous Spectator," in Philip Simpson, Andrew Utterson, and Karen J. Shepherdson, eds., *Film Theory: Critical Concepts in Media and Cultural Studies* (Taylor and Francis, 2004), 78–95.

8 Wolfgang Schivelbusch, *The Railway Journey: The Industrialization of Time and Space in the 19th Century* (University of California Press, 1977), 20.

9 Maxim Gorky, "The Lumière Cinematograph" (1896), reprinted in "Life Devoid of Words," *Lapham's Quarterly*, https://www.laphamsquarterly.org/arts-letters/life-devoid-words.

10 This apocryphal anecdote is recounted in Nafis Shafizadeh's "Gorky at the Movies," *Agni* 92 (2020): 230–35.

11 Robert Daudelin, "Introduction," in 50 *Years of Film Archives* (FIAF, 1988), 8–9, citation on 9.

12 The shot is a combination of live action and computer graphics, all in service of a nostalgic image of early twentieth-century Paris. However seamless the execution, the bravura exhibition of digital cinema mastery, intensified in 3D theatrical exhibition, asserts the place of contemporary digital effects as the successor to early trick cinema à la Méliès. As Kristen Whissel notes, the spectacular nature of this long take comprises much of what distinguishes hybrid forms of digital filmmaking: The "computer-generated (or digitally enhanced) image . . . does not precisely 'arrest' or 'prevail over' narrative but instead appears at key turning points in a film's narrative to emblematize the major themes, desires, and anxieties with which a film (or a group of films) is obsessed." See Kristen Whissel, *Spectacular Digital Effects: CGI and Contemporary Cinema* (Duke University Press, 2014), 6.

13 Vega notes how a child, after watching Anthony Page's 1979 remake of *The Lady Vanishes*, noticed that "people disappear here and no-one says anything." Subsequently the person who had booked the room to Vega was interrogated by the authorities. Alicia Vega, *Taller de cinema para niños* (Ocho Libros, 2011), 97, cited by Sarah Wright, "Child, Cinema, Dictatorship: Ignacio Agüero's *One Hundred Children Waiting for a Train*," in Stephanie Hemelryk Donald, Emma Wilson, and Sarah Wright, eds., *Childhood and Nation in Contemporary World Cinema: Borders and Encounters* (Bloomsbury, 2017), 103–18, citation on 108.

14 Frantz Fanon, *Black Skin, White Masks* (1952), trans. Charles Lam Markmann (Pluto Books, 2008), 107.

15 See Kara Keeling, "'In the Interval': Frantz Fanon and the Problem of Visual Representation," *Qui Parle* 13, no. 2 (Spring–Summer 2003); and Keeling, *The Witch's Flight: The Cinematic, the Black Femme, and the Image of Common Sense* (Duke University Press, 2007).

1. How It Feels to Be a Woman on a Train

1 Lynne Kirby, *Parallel Tracks: The Railroad and Silent Cinema* (Duke University Press, 1997), 77–82.

2 See Laura Mulvey, "Visual Pleasure and the Narrative Cinema," *Screen* 16, no. 3 (1995), reprinted in Laura Mulvey, *Visual and Other Pleasures* (Palgrave Macmillan, 2009), 14–26.

3 Karen Redrobe (Beckman), *Vanishing Women: Magic, Film, and Feminism* (Duke University Press, 2003), 49.
4 L. Frank Baum, *The Art of Decorating Dry Goods Windows and Interiors: A Complete Manual of Window Trimming, Designed as an Educator in all the Details of the Art, According to the Best Accepted Methods, and Treating Fully Every Important Subject* (The Show Window Publishing Company, 1900), 82.
5 Anne Friedberg, *Window Shopping: Cinema and the Postmodern* (University of California Press, 1993), 68.
6 Friedberg, *Window Shopping*, 65.
7 There are some interesting parallels between *Anna Karenina* and the real-life story of Faten Hamama. Like Anna, Hamama was positioned between an older and a younger man. Hamama was married to Ezz El-Dine Zulficar, the film's director, whom she had met while filming *Abu Azyd el-Hilali*, from 1947. They divorced in 1954, and a year later she married the much younger Omar Sharif. Hamama and Sharif starred in many films together, but *The River of Love* (1960) was the last they shot before they, too, were divorced.
8 Wolfgang Schivelbusch, *The Railway Journey: The Industrialization of Time and Space in the 19th Century* (University of California Press, 1977), 54.
9 Extending this logic further, Friedberg asserts that people became commodities. This accords with Karl Marx's suggestion that, in the factory, people were reduced to the status of machine, or even something lower: a "living appendage." See Friedberg, *Window Shopping*, 56; and Karl Marx, *Capital*, Vol. 2, in *Marx Engels Werke* (Dietz, 1956–1990) 24:60; 23:445.
10 Slowpokeking, "Different Versions of Anna Karenina Train Deaths," 2015: https://www.youtube.com/watch?v=G-uRIOFrmO4.

2. Ends of the Line

1 Wolfgang Schivelbusch, *The Railway Journey: The Industrialization of Time and Space in the 19th Century* (University of California Press, 1977), 21.
2 Lynne Kirby, *Parallel Tracks: The Railroad and Silent Cinema* (Duke University Press, 1997), 6, 110.
3 Schivelbusch, *The Railway Journey*, 21, 20.

4 See r/trains, "Which Film Last Made You Point Out an Inconsistency with Trains?," https://www.reddit.com/r/trains/comments/16iv67z/which_film_last_made_you_point_out_an/.

5 See r/trains, "What are Your Opinions/Thoughts on the Snowpiercer Train?," https://www.reddit.com/r/trains/comments/1e6426m/what_are_your_opinionsthoughts_on_the_snowpiercer/.

6 Fatimah Tobing Rony, *The Third Eye: Race, Cinema, and Ethnographic Spectacle* (Duke University Press, 1996), 111; See also Michelle H. Raheja, "Reading Nanook's Smile: Visual Sovereignty, Indigenous Revisions of Ethnography, and *Atanarjuat: The Fast Runner*," in M. Elise Marubbio and Eric L. Buffalohead, eds., *Native Americans on Film: Conversations, Teaching, and Theory* (University Press of Kentucky, 2013).

7 See John F. Stover, *American Railroads* (University of Chicago Press, 1965), 269.

8 Scott Berridge, "Railroads: Old Industry Still Vital in Today's Economy," *Monthly Labor Review*, January 2015, https://www.bls.gov/opub/mlr/2015/beyond-bls/railroads-old-industry-still-vital-in-todays-economy.htm#:~:text=By%20discarding%20miles%20of%20unprofitable,as%20in%20the%20mid%2D1960s.

9 See John Stilgoe, *The Life and Decline of the American Railroad*, 1970, 261, cited in Kirby, *Parallel Tracks*, 78.

10 Alice Diop, "Alice Diop in Conversation with Claire Denis," trans. Catherine Wheatley, *Sight and Sound* (March 2023): 35–42, citation on 37.

Itinerary: Los Angeles to Rhinecliff

1 See Catherine Boland Erkkila, "American Railways and the Cultural Landscape of Immigration," in *Buildings & Landscapes: Journal of the Vernacular Architecture Forum* 22, no. 1 (Spring 2015): 36–62.

2 See Malcolm X, *The Autobiography of Malcolm X* (Ballantine Books, 2015 [1964]), esp. 74–86.

3 Miko Revereza, *Toward a Stateless Cinema* (Hardworking Goodlooking, 2019), 7; See also Feng-Mei Heberer's discussion of Revereza's work in *Asians on Demand: Mediating Race in Video Art and Activism* (University of Minnesota Press, 2023).

4 Revereza, *Toward a Stateless Cinema*, 8.

5 Revereza, *Toward a Stateless Cinema*, 10.

3. Phantom Rides

1 Sigmund Freud, *The Interpretation of Dreams: The Complete and Definitive Text*, trans. James Strachey (Basic Books, 2010 [1899]), 396.

2 James Benning, with Mark Peranson, "Interviews | Trainspotting with James Benning," *Cinemascope* (Spring 2008), https://cinema-scope.com/cinema-scope-magazine/interviews-trainspotting-with-james-benning/.

3 Allan Sekula, "RR JB," in Barbara Pichler and Claudia Slanar, eds. *James Benning* (Synema Publikationen, 2007), 238–40, citation on 239.

4 Sekula, "RR JB," 240.

Itinerary. Shanghai to Hong Kong

1 Chantal Akerman in *Train et cinéma*, Ciné regards television program, France 3, 1981, trans. Daniella Shreir.

2 See also Sierra Pettengill, dir., *Bridges, Trains and Ships* (2017) about Farocki's Bedtime Stories series.

3 Fritz Lang quoted in Frederick W. Ott, *The Films of Fritz Lang* (Citadel Press, 1979). The same citation appears in Tom Gunning, *The Films of Fritz Lang: Allegories of Vision and Modernity* (Bloomsbury Publishing, 2019), 133.

4 Tiffany Sia, *On and Off-Screen Imaginaries* (Primary Information, 2024), 147.

5 Sia, *On and Off-Screen Imaginaries*, 130.

4. Strangers on Trains

1 Lynne Kirby, *Parallel Tracks: The Railroad and Silent Cinema* (Duke University Press, 1997), 82.

2 Brad Stevens, "Mikio Naruse's Wife: Married to the Mainstream," *Sight and Sound*, October 23, 2017, https://www.bfi.org.uk/sight-and-sound/features/mikio-naruses-wife-married-mainstream.

List of Figures

Page 11. Train wreck at Gare Montparnasse, October 22, 1895. Photograph by Studio Lévy.
Page 14. *One Hundred Children Waiting for a Train* (Ignacio Agüero, 1988).
Page 20. *News from Home* (Chantal Akerman, 1976).
Page 29. *Anna Karenina* (Clarence Brown, 1935).
Page 32. *Compartment No. 6* (Juho Kuosmanen, 2021).
Page 35. *The Souvenir* (Joanna Hogg, 2019).
Page 48. *The Iron Horse* (John Ford, 1924).
Page 55. *Bread Day* (Sergei Dvortsevoy, 1998).
Page 58. *35 Shots of Rum* (Claire Denis, 2008).
Page 68. *No Data Plan* (Miko Revereza, 2019).
Page 75. *Brief Encounter* (David Lean, 1945).
Page 79. *Café Lumière* (Hou Hsiao-Hsien, 2003).
Page 87. RR (James Benning, 2007).
Page 96. *A Child Already Knows* (Tiffany Sia, 2025).
Page 98. *Strangers on a Train* (Alfred Hitchcock, 1951).
Page 105. *Distance* (Hirokazu Kore-eda, 2001).
Page 109. *Wife* (Mikio Naruse, 1953).

Index

13 *LAKES* (Benning), 85
35 Shots of Rum (Denis), 57–60
39 Steps, The (Hitchcock), 100
2046 (Wong), 100

accidents, 10, 49, 51, 72, 83. *See also* collision; derailment
After Life (Kore-eda), 103, 106
Akerman, Chantal, 3, 18–19, 21, 91; *News from Home*, 18–21
All That Passes by through a Window That Doesn't Open (Dicicco), 51
Amtrak, 62–63, 65, 86
Andersen, Thom, 87
Anderson, Wes, 3
Anna Karenina (Brown), 27
Anna Karenina (Duvivier), 26
Anna Karenina (Tolstoy), 25–26, 29, 115n7
Anna Karenina (Wright), 27
Arrival of a Train at the Station (Lumière), 2–3, 6–7, 12, 87
Aum Shinrikyo, 103

Baby's Breakfast (Lumière), 8
Barbie (Gerwig), 40
Baum, L. Frank: *The Art of Decorating Dry Goods Windows and Interiors*, 24
Bedtime Stories: Railways (Farocki), 92
Before Midnight (Linklater), 101
Before Sunrise (Linklater), 101
Benning, James, 85–88; *13 LAKES*, 85; *casting a glance*, 85; *RR*, 85–88; *TEN SKIES*, 85
Big Swallow, The (Williamson), 81
Biometrics (Revereza), 69–70
Blind Chance, (Kieślowski), 80–82
borders, 52, 67–68, 70, 92. *See also* immigration
boredom, 63, 67
Bread Day (Dvortsevoy), 54–57
Brief Encounter (Lean), 73–76
Burning Train, The (Chopra), 42–43

Café Lumière, (Hou), 77–80
Calamity (Chytilová), 21–22, 42
camera dolly, 3
Cassandra Crossing, The (Cosmatos), 43

casting a glance (Benning), 85
Child Already Knows, A (Sia), 92–96
childhood, 91; in *A Child Already Knows*, 93–94; Deferred Action for Childhood Arrivals (DACA) Act, 62, 69; Alice Diop on, 59. *See also* children
children: and *Bedtime Stories: Railways*, 92; in *Hugo*, 8; in *Killer of Sheep*, 4; in *One Hundred Children Waiting for a Train*, 12–16; in *Railway Sleepers*, 53; in *RR*, 89
Clouds of Sils Maria (Assayas), 22
collision, 10, 12. *See also* accidents; derailment
community, 64–65. *See also* social mixing
Company's in Love, The (Ophuls), 38
Compartment No. 6 (Kuosamen), 31–33
continuity editing, 3, 42; errors in, 44
Contempt (Godard), 3

Daudelin, Robert, 9
Dead Man (Jarmusch), 63
DeKolta, Alice, 24
DeKolta, Buatier, 24
democracy, 15, 45, 63, 98
derailment, 1, 10, 83
desire: in *Anna Karenina*, 28, 29; for authenticity, 47; in *Possessed*, 2; specular, 27; in *Unfaithful*, 30. *See also* eroticism; love
Dickens, Charles: "The Signal-Man," 72
Diop, Alice, 59–61; *Nous*, 59–61
Distance (Kore-eda), 103–7
documentary, 4, 15, 40, 54, 56, 59, 65, 69, 103
dreams: Chantal Akerman on, 91; anxiety, 80; in *Bedtime Stories: Railways*, 92; in *Café Lumière*, 78; in *A Child Already Knows*, 96; in *Hugo*, 10; in *No Data Plan*, 66; in *Possessed*, 2; in *Valse Triste*, 91–92; in *Woman in the Moon*, 93. *See also* desire; fantasy; sleep
Dumbo (Sharpsteen), 43
duration: in *RR*, 85–86
dust: in *Arrival of a Train at the Station*, 7; in *Compartment No. 6*, 31; in *Distance*, 104; in *The Hero*, 103; as metaphor, 4, 5

eroticism: in *Clouds of Sils Maria*, 22; in Hitchcock, 100; in *Unfaithful*, 30; in *What Happened in the Tunnel*, 100. *See also* desire; romance

Fanon, Frantz: *Black Skin, White Masks*, 15
fantasy: in *A Child Already Knows*, 92; in *The Company's*

in Love, 38; in *From Mayerling to Sarajevo*, 38; in *The Hero*, 103; in *The Souvenir*, 36; in *What Happened in the Tunnel*, 100. *See also* desire
fate, 8, 27, 38, 80
feminism: as method, 5–6
Flavor of Green Tea over Rice, The (Ozu), 30–31
Ford, John, 5, 45, 47; *The Iron Horse*, 45–48; *The Man Who Shot Liberty Vance*, 45
freedom, 65, 70
Freud, Sigmund, 80
Friedberg, Anne, 24–25, 115n9
From Mayerling to Sarajevo (Ophuls), 38

Geyserland (Strom), 89
Ghost Train, The (Forde), 72
glass, 4, 18; in *Anna Karenina*, 30; in *Calamity*, 21–22, 24–26; in *Compartment No. 6*, 31, 32, 33; in *Hugo*, 10; in *The Lady Vanishes*, 17. *See also* reflection; windows
Glazar, Richard, 41
Godard, Jean-Luc, 3; *Contempt*, 3
Gorky, Maxim, 7–8, 72
Great Train Robbery, The (Porter), 3, 5
Gunning, Tom, 6
Guthrie, Woody: "This Land is Your Land," 88–89

Hero, The (Ray), 101–3
Hitchcock, Alfred, 17, 35, 97, 99–100; *The 39 Steps*, 100; *The Lady Vanishes*, 17–18, 100; *North by Northwest*, 63, 100; *Rope*, 100; *Saboteur*, 100; *Spellbound*, 100; *Strangers on a Train*, 97–100; *Suspicion*, 100; *Vertigo*, 35, 36–37
Hugo (Scorsese), 8–12, 13

immigration, 59, 62, 64. *See also* borders; movement; *No Data Plan*
imposters: in *No Man of Her Own*, 84; plot, 84
In Transit (Maysles), 65
Incredibles, The (Bird), 43
intimacy: in *A Child Already Knows*, 96; in *Clouds of Sils Maria*, 22; in *The Souvenir*, 36. *See also* eroticism; romance
Iron Horse, The (Ford), 45–48
Iron Ministry, The (Sniadecki), 4

Jay Kelly (Baumbach), 102

Keeling, Kara, 15
Killer of Sheep (Burnett), 4
Kirby, Lynne, 1, 20, 41, 99

labor, 43, 44, 47. *See also* railway workers
Lady Vanishes, The (Hitchcock), 17–18, 100
Lang, Fritz, 93

Last Days of Disco, The (Stillman), 73
Lean, David, 5, 73; *Brief Encounter*, 73–76
Leave Her to Heaven (Stahl), 100
Letter from an Unknown Woman (Ophuls), 37–39
love: in *Anna Karenina*, 26, 28; in *Brief Encounter*, 73; in *From Mayerling to Sarajevo*, 38; in *The Last Days of Disco*, 73; in *Letter from an Unknown Woman*, 37; in *No Man of Her Own*, 84; in *Sliding Doors*, 80; in *The Souvenir*, 34, 36
Lumière, Auguste, 2, 6–8, 12; *Arrival of a Train at the Station*, 2–3, 6–7, 12, 87
Lumière, Louis, 2, 6–8, 12; *Arrival of a Train at the Station*, 2–3, 6–7, 12, 87; *Baby's Breakfast*, 8

male gaze, the, 20, 108
Man Who Shot Liberty Vance, The (Ford), 45
Mangolte, Babette, 18
Marey, Étienne-Jules, 3
Marx, Karl, 115n9
Masstransiscope (Brand), 89–90
Méliès, Georges, 8–12, 24, 114n12; *The Vanishing Lady*, 24
memory, 6; in *Blind Chance*, 82; in *A Child Already Knows*, 92, 94; in *Distance*, 104, 105; in *Hugo*, 9; in *The Souvenir*, 38; in *Still Life*, 74
Mizoguchi, Kenzo, 3
modernity, 1, 42, 51
mood: in *35 Shots of Rum*, 58; in *Distance*, 104; in *Tickets*, 6
movement: in *Arrival of a Train at the Station*, 10; in *Masstransiscope*, 90; of motion pictures, 12, 69, 90; and trains, 6–7, 25, 93
Mulvey, Laura, 22
murder: in *The Commuter*, 43; in *Murder on the Orient Express*, 63; plot, 97, 99; in *Strangers on a Train*, 97, 99; in *Unfaithful*, 30
Murder on the Orient Express (Christie), 63
Muybridge, Eadweard, 3

News from Home (Akerman), 18–21
Newton, Isaac, 40
Night Mail (Wright and Watt), 27
Night Train (Kawalerowicz), 100
No Data Plan (Revereza), 62–63, 65–69
No Man of Her Own (Leisen), 83–84
North by Northwest (Hitchcock), 63, 100
nostalgia: in *Hugo*, 114n12; and trains, 92. *See also* childhood; memory
Nous (Diop), 59–61

One Hundred Children Waiting for a Train (Agüero), 12–16

Ophuls, Max, 37, 38; *Company's in Love, The*, 38; *From Mayerling to Sarajevo*, 38; *Letter from an Unknown Woman*, 37–39
Ozu, Yasujirō, 5, 31, 77; *The Flavor of Green Tea over Rice*, 30–31

parcels, 27, 40
perspective: in *Blind Chance*, 82; in *Compartment No. 6*, 32; in *Possessed*, 2; in *The Power of Kangwon Province*, 76; train, 71–72, 78, 89. *See also* trains: POV
phantom ride, 3, 71–72. *See also* perspective: train; trains: POV
Possessed (Brown), 1–2, 27
Power of Kangwon Province, The (Hong), 76–77

railroad: construction of, 45–47, 51; history of, 45, 52
Railroad Smashup (Edison), 72
Railway Sleepers (Chidgasornpongse), 52–53
railway workers, 26, 41, 48, 49, 57. *See also* labor
Ray, Satyajit, 3, 101; *The Hero*, 101–3
Red Eye (Dong-bin), 72
Redrobe, Karen, 24
reflection, 5, 18, 22; in *Anna Karenina*, 29; in *Blind Chance*, 82; in *No Man of Her Own*, 83
revolution, 4
River of Love, The (Zulficar), 25–26, 115n7
romance: in *Before Sunrise*, 101; in *Brief Encounter*, 73; in *Café Lumière*, 78; and trains, 4, 99–101. *See also* eroticism; intimacy
Rope (Hitchcock), 100
RR (Benning), 85–88
Runaway Train (Konchalovsky), 42

Saboteur (Hitchcock), 100
Saint Omer (Diop), 60
Schivelbusch, Wolfgang, 6, 26, 40, 98
segregation, 64, 98
Sekula, Allan, 86, 88
Shang-Chi (Cretton), 43
Shoah (Lanzmann), 40–41
Sia, Tiffany, 92, 94–96; *A Child Already Knows*, 92–96; *On and Offscreen Imaginaries*, 94
silent film, 2, 9
sleep: in *Anna Karenina*, 28; Sigmund Freud on, 80; in *The Iron Ministry*, 4; in *Jay Kelly*, 102; in *Railway Sleepers*, 53; in *The River of Love*, 25; in *Take the 5:10 to Dreamland*, 92. *See also* dreams
Sliding Doors (Howitt), 80
smoothness, 40, 42, 45
Snowpiercer (Joon-Ho), 43–45
social mixing, 98

Some Like it Hot (Wilder), 63
Source Code (Jones), 43
Souvenir, The (Hogg), 34, 38
Souvenir Part II, The (Hogg), 38
spectacle: in *Arrival of a Train at the Station*, 7
Spellbound (Hitchcock), 100
Spirited Away (Miyazake), 72
Stanford, Leland, 3, 46
Stanwyck, Barbara, 6, 33, 83
Stella Dallas (Vidor), 33
Stevens, Brad, 108
Still Life (Coward), 74
strangers, 90; in *Distance*, 106; and eroticism, 100; in *The Hero*, 103; in *Strangers on a Train*, 97, 99–100; in *In Transit*, 65; in *What Happened in the Tunnel*, 100. *See also* social mixing
Strangers on a Train (Hitchcock), 97–100
subway, the, 42, 103; in *Café Lumière*, 79; in *The Last Days of Disco*, 73; and *Masstransiscope*, 89; in *News from Home*, 18–19, 21
suicide: in *35 Shots of Rum*, 58; in *Anna Karenina*, 29; in *Clouds of Sils Maria*, 23; in *Distance*, 106; in Maxim Gorky's short story, 8; in *Still Life*, 76
Sullivan's Travels (Sturges), 63
Suspicion (Hitchcock), 100
Take the 5:10 to Dreamland (Conner), 92
Taking of Pelham 1 2 3, The (Sargent), 42
TEN SKIES (Benning), 85
Throw Momma from the Train (DeVito), 99–100
This Is the Way I Like It (Agüero), 15
Tickets (Olmi et al), 6
time: in *All That Passes by Through a Window that Doesn't Open*, 52; in RR, 85. *See also* duration
tracking shot: early, 3; in *Calamity*, 21
trailers, 3
trains: American, 63–64; enthusiasts, 44, 72; as film's "mechanical double," 1; ideology of, 40; invention of, 26; and masculinity, 20; mechanical reality of, 42; as motif, 2, 80; as narrative catalyst, 44; POV, 72, 82, 85; and race, 64; sounds of, 77, 88; women on, 30. *See also* subway, the
Train, The (Frankenheimer), 43
Train to Busan (Sang-ho), 43
Tscherkassky, Peter, 87
Tukunen, Taïna, 4

Unfaithful (Lyne), 30
Unstoppable (Scott), 49

V for Vendetta (McTeigue), 43
Valse Triste (Conner), 91–92
Vanishing Lady, The (Méliès), 24
Vanishing Lady, The (Paul), 24
Vertigo (Hitchcock), 35, 36–37

waiting: in *35 Shots of Rum*, 57; in *Black Skin, White Masks*, 15; in *Bread Day*, 55; in *Calamity*, 21–22; and immigration, 64; in *RR*, 86
war, 45, 56, 88, 93
western, the, 3. *See also* Ford, John
What Happened in the Tunnel (Dickson), 100
Whissel, Kristen, 114n12
White Noise (Baumbach), 51
Wife (Naruse), 107–9
windows, 1, 4, 94; in *Anna Karenina*, 26–28; in *Bedtime Stories: Railways*, 92; in *Café Lumière*, 78; in *Calamity*, 21–22; in *Compartment No. 6*, 32; in *Dead Man*, 63; display, 24–25, 96; in *The Lady Vanishes*, 17–18; in *Letter from an Unknown Woman*, 37; as metaphor, 6, 25; in *News from Home*, 18, 19, 21; in *No Data Plan*, 66, 67; in *Railway Sleepers*, 52, 53; in *RR*, 86; in *Stella Dallas*, 33; view, 1, 6, 90, 91, 107, 109. *See also* glass; perspective; reflection
Woman in the Moon (Lang), 93
women: desiring, 29; doubling, 84; as images, 25; looking, 20, 22, 29; riding, 27; thinking, 29, 30; vanishing, 24, 109; waiting, 55. *See also* feminism

Žižek, Slavoj, 2

Genevieve Yue is Associate Professor of Culture and Media and Director of Screen Studies at Eugene Lang College, The New School. She is the author of *Girl Head: Feminism and Film Materiality* (2021). Her writing has appeared in *October*, *Grey Room*, *Film Comment*, *MUBI*, and the *Times Literary Supplement*. She is also an independent film programmer.

CUTAWAYS

SERIES EDITORS:
Erika Balsom and **Genevieve Yue**

Elena Gorfinkel, John David Rhodes, *The Prop*

Jules O'Dwyer, *Hotels*

Martine Beugnet (translated by Lindsay Turner), *Blur*

Genevieve Yue, *Trains*